A Photographer's Guide to
the Safari Experience

Photos and Text by
Todd Gustafson

In Memory of Paul Gustafson
1921-2008

Cover photo. Bull elephant in Ngorongoro Crater, Tanzania

Common zebras, Maasai Mara, Kenya

Reticulated giraffe, Samburu National Reserve, Kenya

A Photographer's Guide to
the Safari Experience

By Todd Gustafson

AN ON LOCATION GUIDE

MONOGRAPH
PUBLISHING

A Photographer's Guide to the Safari Experience
by Todd Gustafson

Published By: Monograph Publishing, LLC
1 Putt Lane
Eureka, Missouri 63025
636.938.1100
Email: info@mathisjones.com

Web site: gustafsonphotosafari.net
Library of Congress Catalogue-in-Publication Data: On File

ISBN: 978-0-9799482-1-3

Printed in the United States of America
09 10 11 12 01   5 4 3 2 1

CONTENTS

SAFARI TALES

SIDE BARS

APPENDIX

Dedication

I want to dedicate this book to all the people who have been so generous and supportive in my photographic development. The information contained in this book is the result of 20 years of photographing East Africa.

First on the list, and most important, are my parents, Paul and Louise Gustafson, who had the courage to move a family of 5 to East Africa to build a school for East African boys. My father's knowledge of biology and zoology coupled with his interest in photography have been an inspiration to me for years.

Thanks to my older brother and best friend Brian Gustafson with whom I have spent countless hours discussing the fine points of safari itineraries. His knowledge of indigenous people and the culture of East Africa has helped immeasurably when working with people "on the ground".

When my wife owned the only camera in the house, a Canon Sure Shot, it was my friend Mike Sergey who told me to get something called an SLR. My first question was "What's an f-stop?" My mother-in-law, Lois Stenstrom, gave me a Nikon N2000 as a birthday gift so I could take "professional" pictures on my first safari in 1986.

In 1997 it was Mike Sergey again who told me that Nikon now had a camera body called the F5. I took that with a Sigma 170-500mm lens and the photography started in earnest. Thank you Mike!

Defassa water buck, Crescent Island, Lake Naivasha, Kenya

Thanks to Tom Tyler who has been friend and supporter from the beginning. My first big project was with Tom, placing East African images in the St. Louis Children's Memorial Hospital.

Another friend who has been indispensable in his support, knowledge, and honesty is Robert Lightfoot. Photographer of the Chicago Symphony Orchestra during the Sir Georg Solti years, he has continually pushed me to see beyond my current vision to the next level.

In 1997 I traveled to Kenya with Arthur Morris, the world's premier bird photographer. The techniques and vision I learned from him have stayed with me ever since. His friendship and advice have helped propel me into a full time nature photography career. I am continually striving to keep up with his pioneering work in digital nature photography.

Lastly I would like to give my deepest thanks and love to my wife Julie and my children, Dana, Jeni, and Anders. They are the ones who have allowed me to pursue the dream of nature photography. The time spent away from them is difficult for me but I try to take them with me whenever I can. Because of this, I think they know how important this whole thing is to me. The reunions after a safari keep our lives and relationships fresh and meaningful.

"Thanks, and I love you madly!"

Prologue

My Best Images from the 1997 Safari

Safari Tale #1

I took some pictures that I liked in 1997 on a family safari. I mailed the best ones to an out-of-town film lab. When they came back, the prints were crushed and the negatives lost. How depressing! My understanding wife said "Just go back and get better pictures."

Later that week I got a chance to shoot Sigma Lens Corporation's new 800mm f5.6 lens in Florida. I had no idea where to go for pictures in Florida so I went out on a limb and called internationally renowned bird photographer, Arthur Morris.
I had been told that he knew the best Florida spots.
He asked me what I liked to photograph.
"East Africa" I said.
"East Africa!?" He said... "I'm going to East Africa."
I remembered my wife's suggestion to "Just go back and get better pictures." "So am I!" I replied "Who are you going with?"
"I don't know," he said.
"Neither do I," I replied.
He said, "You show me the best places to photograph birds and I'll teach you everything I know about photography."
Talk about a life changing moment! We went to Kenya for 4 weeks and for 12 hours a day Arthur patiently instructed, encouraged and quizzed me on nature photography. I will be forever grateful to this generous and giving man.
(He also told me where to photograph in Florida)

Lesson: "Success is 90% just showing up." Woody Allen

Left: The beginning of a journey, Hell's Gate National Park, Kenya

Savannah biome, Maasai Mara, Kenya

Introduction

The first thing that you should know about this book is that it is not a photography book. It does not deal with technical discussions of the latest camera and electronic gear. There is an assumption here that you have good quality camera equipment and that you understand how it works. You know basic photographic theory and understand the concepts of digital photography.

The very word safari brings to mind images of jungles and savannahs teaming with birds and animals. Exotic natives share the land with lions, elephants and herds of zebras. This romantic view of East Africa coexists in some places with the modern East Africa of today. Understanding elements of both worlds will make for a richer, more rewarding experience for all who are fortunate enough to go on safari. This book discusses the practical aspects of undertaking a photographic safari.

One of its purposes is to provide information that will be valuable to a photographer dealing with the unique situations encountered on an East African safari. Familiarity with such diverse issues as travel, food, lodging, safari vehicles, and the weather (to name just a few) can relieve pre-trip anxiety and the stress of encountering new situations while traveling. This book will teach you how to pack appropriately so that both you and your camera gear will arrive safely.

Information shared here can help you make choices that can help you realize your artistic vision to the best of your ability. Learning the techniques to photograph from a safari vehicle will dramatically improve your results. In the text boxes you will learn from real life photographic experiences.

Having grown up in Tanzania, I view the "African Experience" from the inside. My family lived in the Usambara Mountains where my father built and was headmaster (1962-1965) of the Magamba Secondary School. During the past two decades I have escorted more than 200 people on photographic safaris to East Africa.

The primary focus of this book is to help you learn to create engaging photographs of the interesting and dynamic subjects you will encounter on a photographic safari.

Preparing to Photograph on Safari

Digital Photographic Equipment

Safari photography has specialized needs and therefore requires specialized equipment. The list of recommended gear is something that each safari traveler needs to consider; they must take into account their photographic style, their budget, the equipment they own, and air line baggage and carry-on allowances.

A few years ago we would have been discussing the merits of the Nikon F5 camera body versus the Canon EOS 1V. We agonized over the different grain structures of the various Fujichrome and Kodachrome films and how many stops they could be push-processed. Panoramic 6x17 cameras and 6x7 large format cameras sometimes found their way into the camera bags along with dozens or even hundreds of rolls of film. We now live in the digital camera age, where file size, lens conversion factors and megapixels rule. I am not going to discuss the merits of one camera system over another or the notion that one camera body is better than another. By the time you read the next sentence, this or that that camera body would be obsolete. What I will discuss is the physical act of taking and using a digital camera system on a photographic safari.

Assume that you have a camera body that you like. Next, assume that your camera will malfunction or quit working completely while you are on safari. It is imperative that you travel with a back-up camera body. Some travel with a similar but less expensive camera. Their rationale is that they will use their back-up body only on short lenses (and as a back up if need be, since most of their photography will be done with their long lens and their main camera body).

Others bring two identical camera bodies so both cameras will have the same control buttons no matter which lens choice they make. In an emergency they will still have one functioning version of their favorite camera body.

Another school of thought is to have three bodies. That way if one goes down you can still shoot two bodies without changing lenses. The considerations at this point include your budget, the limitations of your packing space, and airline weight allowances.

Cleaning Digital Sensors

Safari photography is a dusty endeavor, so traveling with a sensor cleaning kit is mandatory (even for those with cameras that have built-in sensor cleaning capabilities). Digital camera sensors need to be cleaned even in the best studio conditions; on safari the dust can drive you to distraction. The best way that I have found to clean the sensor is with a product called the Lens Pen®. The composite, felt-like, flat tip is coated with carbon powder stored in the pen's cap. Clean the powder from the tip by tapping it repeatedly on a clean micro-fiber cloth prior to cleaning the sensor.

Next, hold the shutter open. This is done differently with different camera systems so you need to consult your camera body manual. Use a blower brush to blow out the loose particles. (Do not use canned air. It may blow dirt under the sensor cover). Then rub the tip of the Lens Pen rather firmly over the entire surface of the sensor. The composite tip usually picks up all of the dust and grit on one pass. Lastly, blow out the chamber again and close the shutter. When you change lenses additional dust may work its way onto the sensor.

Image Capture

Capturing digital images on safari is done almost universally on compact flash or SD cards. Many companies manufacture them. Issues that affect your choice of cards include their reliability, the number of gigabytes (and images) that can be stored on the card, the write speed, and your personal shooting style.

At this point (and again, tomorrow the situation will be different) either 12 or 16gb cards are large enough to hold the sometimes huge image files produced by the higher end digital cameras. I like the SanDisc Extreme III cards because of their fast write speeds and their dependability. I have never had to deal with a corrupted SanDisc card…

Image Storage

Image storage devices come in all shapes, sizes and price ranges. Files can be downloaded onto these devices and edited in the field or at home. Storage choices include: multiple compact flash cards, portable external hard drives, and laptop computers.

Some amateur photographers choose to travel only with compact flash and SD cards and keep all of their images on the cards. They use JPEG capture as these files are tiny compared with the RAW files that used by nearly all serious photographers. They can fit thousands of JPEG images on a single card and make even more room by deleting images with obvious and serious flaws.

All serious photographers are advised to create the largest possible RAW files. Such RAW files contain more image data than any JPEGs. In addition, they produce images that feature less contrast than JPEGs and allow the photographer to correct even gross exposure or White Balance errors. Most pro camera bodies have options to include a JPEG along with each RAW file. I use the "RAW plus JPEG BASIC" option on my D3 bodies for quick and easy editing. My editing program (BreezeBrowser Pro) quickly views the small JPEG. If I choose to delete that image the RAW file is automatically deleted as well. Serious photographers using RAW capture will make many thousands of images on a typical safari, so storage space is a critical concern.

For folks traveling with laptop computers, portable external hard drives can provide ample storage space even for the most serious photographers; they currently range in size from 160-500gbs, and they are getting cheaper every month. Whatever your external storage capabilities, it is important to edit your images daily so that your laptop computer has enough free space to operate efficiently; if you have no means of editing your images, problems are unavoidable.

Another storage option is to travel with one of the many image dump tanks that are available. These allow image files to be downloaded directly from the flash card to the storage device. Some of the more sophisticated dump tank storage devices have editing windows so that the photographer can view image thumbnails; images can then be deleted. These viewing screens are simply not large enough to meet the critical editing needs of advanced photographers. If you do your editing on a tiny screen it is very possible that you will wind up keeping many sub-par images and deleting many potentially excellent images.

I bring a mid-sized laptop with plenty of storage space and a high quality screen on all safaris. I prefer an 11" screen; my laptop is small enough to be easily transported yet the screen is large enough for me to do my critical editing on the trip. It is my observation that the larger laptop computers take more of a pounding under rigorous travel conditions.

Laptop computers get more powerful by the day. At the time of this writing a computer with a 100 gb hard drive can easily handle the images from a 15 day safari as long as you edit your images every day and delete the rejects. As laptop computers can fail, it is a good idea to have a pocket-sized external hard drive for back up and/or an image dump tank so that you can back up your images. Backing up your images is an absolute necessity.

Some photographers back up their images by burning CDs or DVDs; this solution is an extremely time-consuming one (and assumes that you will have a reliable source of electricity during the evening, which is not always the case on safari).

The solutions to image storage that I recommend are those that will be most efficient, including the use of your time. An African safari is, and should be, more than sitting at your computer editing and backing up your images. Less time spent on your computer allows you to enjoy the experience more fully, as well as be more alert the next day. This will result in better photography.

At this time I use a HYPERDRIVE® to download cards in the field. When I return to the lodge, all of the cards from the shoot are already downloaded so I can begin editing by plugging the drive into my laptop. When I am done editing, I copy and paste the edited set of folders onto the laptop drive. This process has saved hours of downloading time.

Remember, the less time you spend on your computer, the more time you will have to enjoy the safari experience, and you will be more alert the next day.

Software Programs

There are so many programs available to the digital photographer, they can make your head spin. I won't try to review them all for you. These are the main programs I use.

Downloading software

Many top professional photographers use Down Loader Pro from Breeze Systems. This program attaches information to each image as it is downloaded. Date, time, location, subject, photographer, key wording, copyright, and many more key words can be automatically added to each image.

I copy the file folder from the card into my computer library. I have a main folder labeled (for this example) TANZANIA 2008. Inside of that folder will be each day's set of folders labeled by letter.

For this example:

Madagascar A

Madagascar B

Madagascar C

Some people use a numbering system while others use the date. It is important that you have a system that works for you. You must be able to quickly find images that you want. On a typical safari with 15 days of shooting I will have from 40-50 labeled file folders. My best images from each shoot are copied to the folder labeled AAA TZ 08. I can easily access them when I want to work on them.

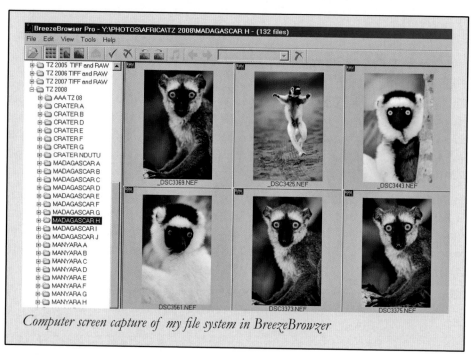

Computer screen capture of my file system in BreezeBrowzer

4

Editing Programs

Once the file folders from the day's shoot are labeled and in place I open the folder in an editing program. There are many editing programs; I use BreezeBrowser Pro because it is extremely fast and because it temporarily sharpens the JPEGs that I am viewing. These JPEGs provide an accurate representation of the RAW images and give me a good idea of what the image will look like after it has been optimized. It is a real plus that BreezeBrowser can handle image files from both Nikon and Canon cameras.

When the folder of images is opened, push "Control-A" to select all the images. Then push "Control-S" to start a slide show of all the images in the folder.

Temporarily sharpened JPEG in BreezeBrowser "slide show" mode

Image files can be viewed by hitting the right arrow key (which is usually located on the right side of the keyboard). To go back and compare an image with the previous one, use the left arrow key. Images can be tagged for deletion by hitting the up arrow key. If you change your mind, you can un-tag an image by hitting the down arrow key. On the first edit, all files that are out of focus, poorly composed, feature poor or harsh light or awkward poses, or otherwise don't make the cut should be deleted. If you have multiple images of a great subject in a great situation, only a few of the best ones should be kept. These will usually be the very sharpest images in the series or those featuring dramatic expressions or perfect head angles.

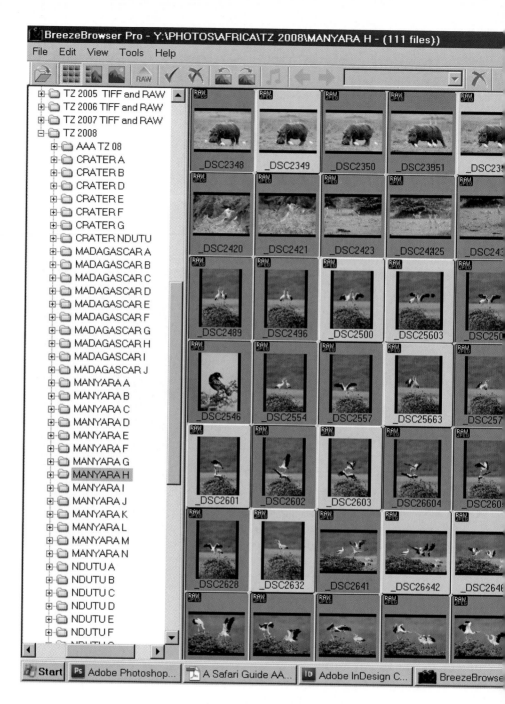

When the slide show is finished, hit "Escape" to exit. Then hit the f6 key to select the tagged images. The rejects will be highlighted; hit the Delete key; the tagged images will be deleted; the remaining images will be your "keepers" from the first edit. On a card with 200 images I will keep an average of 50 on the first edit.

_DSC2357 _DSC2360 _DSC2365 _DSC2376 _DSC2385 _DSC2413
_DSC2464 _DSC2466 _DSC2475 _DSC2478 _DSC2481 _DSC2488
_DSC2513 _DSC2522 _DSC2535 _DSC2536 _DSC2541 _DSC2543
_DSC2578 _DSC2587 _DSC2589 _DSC2598 _DSC2599 _DSC2600
_DSC2608 _DSC2610 _DSC2614 _DSC2620 _DSC2623 _DSC2626
_DSC2654 _DSC2655 _DSC2656 _DSC2661 _DSC2662 _DSC2665

BreezeBrowser... | Screen Capture a....   « 🎲 📇   9:13 AM

7

Showing Images

On the safari there is often time to share and compare images by viewing them on laptop computers. Some groups have a last day "show and tell" where everyone on the safari shows their top 40 or so images. Some folks display the extracted JPEGs that are accurate representations of the RAW files while others show their optimized images. Breeze Browser has a great RAW converter but I prefer to convert my images in Adobe Photoshop's Camera Raw. Slide show JPEGs should be at least 1000 pixels tall and no larger than 100 kbs.

Camera Support

The support system that you use on safari will have a direct effect on image sharpness and therefore on the total number of quality images that you make. As with all photo-related purchases, deciding what equipment you purchase requires a balancing act between what you want versus what you need versus what your budget will allow.

Bean Bags

Bean bags are an economical and simple method of rooftop camera support on safari. The beans effectively kill van vibration and the camera can nestle comfortably in the bag. They work well, if you have ample time to set up for a shot. One drawback is that your rig is not high enough for most folks to shoot comfortably. It is difficult to move a heavy beanbag quickly into position; critical moments may be missed. Bean bags are loose items that have a tendency to be on the floor just when they are needed, causing the photographer to have to bend over to pick them up. Whenever you move on safari, the van shakes, spoiling things for everyone else which may create animosity. I prefer to leave the beanbags at home.

Todd-Pod

The Safari Todd-Pod is a simple T-mount that allows you to mount your big lens on a Wimberley head. It is perfect for use with Land Rover Defenders and safari vans that have three roof hatches. The whole rig can be easily lifted from one side of the vehicle to the other. The Todd-Pod allows a photographer to follow the action easily and enjoy all of the benefits of the Wimberley head. With it, you can even make great flight images from the top of a safari vehicle.

The added height of this set up allows for hours of safari photography without the shoulder and neck pain or back and leg strain that results from the hunched posture associated with shooting off of a beanbag. This added shooting comfort will keep the photographer fresher both mentally and physically and allow them to put more energy into creating beautiful images.

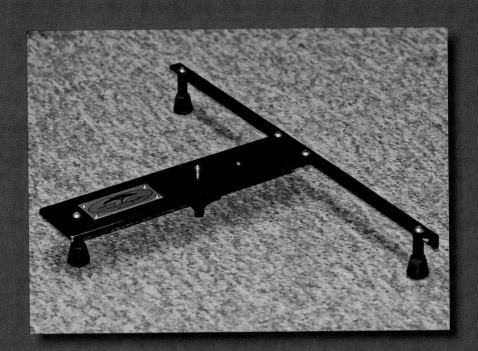

A Todd-Pod is used by many safari photographers.

Tripods

I use a 600mm Nikon lens with a Nikon D3 and a Nikon flash along with the Quantum 2X2 off-camera battery. With all of this gear and the weight of the Wimberley head, it is vital that I use a high quality tripod. For a tall photographer, the Gitzo GT3540XLS is strong enough and tall enough to do even flight photography in total comfort. Folks of average height using either a 500mm lenses or the Nikon 200-400mm f4 lens should go with the Gitzo 3530 LSV tripod. The larger of the two Mongoose heads, the M3.5 is ideal for use with the 200-400.

There are few places to use tripods on safari game drives. Most photography is done from the top of a safari vehicle. Still, there are places where a tripod will enable you to capture spectacular wildlife images. I use mine when visiting the Rift Valley lakes, where birds abound. Hotels and lodges all have opportunities to walk the grounds. Most lodges have feeders where birds are accustomed to people and are easily photographed. A tripod can also be used when photographing from a boat.

Lake Nakuru has areas where you can safely photograph flamingos from outside the vehicle.

Crescent Island in Kenya is a great place for hiking with a long lens and a tripod.

Electric Power and Recharging Equipment

Most cameras use different batteries. Every laptop needs a power supply and a transformer. Many folks use lots of rechargeable AA batteries and still others use external battery packs for their flashes. East Africa uses 220-240 electrical power and most rechargeable electronics now have dual power source capability. This means that if your electronic device has a transformer, it will most likely accept both 110 and 220/240 voltage. To find out if the devices you have fit into this category, look on the label on the transformer for the words "input 100-240."

There are, however, many places in East Africa—whether lodges or camps—where power outlets are scarce. There are just not enough of them to go around when a group of serious digital photographers shows up. This is the reason I build and market the Todd-Plug, originally designed with help from Martin Plant, a photographer from the UK. The Todd-Plug is a power strip designed to fit in East African outlets. It is capable of charging as many as 8 universal plug devices at once. In places with only a single outlet, they can be daisy chained together to provide plenty of spots for everyone's gear. Some devices do not have a universal plug cord. Plug adapters (USA-UK) should be included in an electrical recharging kit for these items.

Some of the lodges and camps use generators to supply the electrical power and the generators usually do not run all day. Generator hours may not always match the times when you are back at the lodge with free time to charge your batteries. Creative rotation of equipment and charging during mealtimes can usually alleviate this problem. Some lodge managers will even alter the hours of operation to accommodate a polite request from a needy photo group.

Health Precautions

Health is an important issue when traveling to any unfamiliar country. Check with your doctor as to which pre-trip inoculations are recommended. You can also check the CDC (Center for Disease Control) web site for complete information on the area to which you are going. You will need a malaria prophylactic. There are several types, so get your doctor's recommendation. Drink only bottled water. Be sure to stay well hydrated (even on your flights). Use bottled water to brush your teeth. Eat cooked vegetables and avoid salads where the ingredients may have been washed with local water.

Safari Tale #2

In January, 2004 Arthur Morris had decided to take a chance and do an entire Tanzania safari with his new digital equipment. Armed with the newest Canon camera bodies, a fist full of compact flash cards and a new Toshiba laptop, Art flew into Kilimanjaro Airport ready for a totally digital safari. He stayed the first night at the Moivaru Plantation where he had a comfortable room with plenty of electrical outlets. Art had drained the batteries on his laptop on the flight from Amsterdam so he was eager to recharge them. But first—in need of nutrition after the long flight—he plugged in his electric hand blender to mix a protein shake; the blender exploded with a large electrical "pop". (Art did not realize that with the 220 voltage he needed a transformer to safely use an electrical appliance in Africa).

Next, Art brought out his store-bought US power strip to begin charging his computers. When he plugged it in the wall socket, there was an ominous "whoof," accompanied by a cute little mushroom cloud of black smoke. At that point, he decided to turn the laptop on with the remaining piece of electrical hardware left to him, a US-UK plug adaptor. His laptop was totally nonfunctional. It had gone into a deep sleep. "Call the airline and get me a ticket home," was heard from one end of Tanzania to the other. After a $100 call to a Toshiba service center in Cuba, he was finally able to boot up the computer. He had a wastebasket full of discarded electrical equipment and the smell of an electrical fire was in the air. Welcome to East Africa.

Lesson: *Know your equipment before you go, and bring a Todd-Plug.*

The Big Five

In the days of the great white hunter the most prized trophies were elephant, rhino, Cape buffalo, lion, and leopard. Caravans of hunters, porters, gun bearers, and supply carts went into the bush looking for the opportunity to bag their prizes. The animals were hunted, shot, stuffed, and mounted. For the safari photographer, the prize still exists. Capturing images of the "Big Five" with a camera and long lens is a more artistic and humane goal. It is a difficult challenge and can produce a feeling of great accomplishment when it is done well... and, you can still get home with something to put over the mantle piece. On some safaris it is possible to photograph the "Big Five." And sometimes it is even possible to photograph the "Big Five" in a single game park.

The most amazing thing I have ever experienced on safari was to view the "Big Five" in the space of ten minutes without moving the van! It happened in Tanzania's Ngorongoro Crater at the Fig Tree picnic area. Our van went to the site early to see if there were any birds in the area before all the vans arrived for breakfast. As we pulled in, we spotted 2 young male lions climbing up into the fig tree. (An hour later there were unsuspecting tourists picnicking under that same tree). As we repositioned the van we saw a black rhino on the lip of the dell. Next, an elephant came out of the marsh to browse on the papyrus as twelve Cape buffalo came in from left of the marsh for a drink. Nobody could figure out what to photograph first. Suddenly the situation was compounded when our driver yelled "leopard!" It had been in the fig tree that was now behind us (and it was the leopard in the tree that had garnered the lions' attention). With the beautiful cat running for the marsh and the two young lions stalking the Cape Buffalo, we decided to try to photograph the leopard, and as a result could only watch as the lions charged the buffalo. One of the lions leaped on a buffalo's back while the panicked animal bucked and kicked, sending the lion rolling into a nearby bush!! When the dust settled things had happened so quickly that no one had photographs of any of the action. The memory, however, will last a lifetime, proving that a good photo safari is more than the sum of your photographs.

Fig Tree picnic site with tourists and lions, Ngorongoro Crater, Tanzania

Transporting Camera Equipment

Packing for safari can be a logistical challenge. A list of what you want to bring on safari and a list of what you need to bring on safari would be two very different lists. When you do the final packing, your carefully selected blend of needs and wants will have to mesh with the weight limits imposed by the airlines.

It is a good idea to find the current guidelines of your chosen airline. Find out how many bags you are allowed to check and note the size and weight limits for these bags. Find out how many bags you are allowed to carry onto the plane and note the allowed sizes and weights of those.

To the right is the carefully chosen and time-tested list of items that I bring with me on safari. See if there are things on the list that you didn't think of. There are most certainly things that you will bring that are not on my list, but you will get a general idea of what is needed on safari. I am very careful when deciding which items I will carry on the plane and which items will be under the plane. The items on page 18 are in red and are always in my carry-on bag(s).

Notice that if none of my checked bags made it to East Africa I would still be able to photograph on safari. I would have all of my essential cameras and lenses, my computer and card readers, as well as my toiletries, medicine, and money.

Packing your camera bag will require special attention. The reason you are traveling to East Africa is, after all, to photograph. This means your photo bag must be packed carefully so that all of the gear you have chosen to bring gets from your house to East Africa in good working order.

I use a rolling camera bag from PELICAN®. It has a detachable computer bag and can function as a one piece bag or an independent rolling case with an over the shoulder computer bag. The first thing I do is remove all of the padded dividers from the case. I pack the 600mm lens in a neoprene bag along one of the case sides. I place the 200-400VR lens against the other side of the case.

Next, I fit all the short lenses and teleconverters in the spaces around the big lenses, each of these in its own small, neoprene bag. I then put the camera bodies across the front top of the bag, each in its own medium sized neoprene bag. There are plenty of small spaces left for other small lenses and cords. Last of all, the chargers are packed. With this system I have everything that I need for a photographic safari on the plane with me.

I keep a mid-sized computer with all the supporting cords and necessary discs in the zip-on computer bag. The Todd Plug fits in there along with the adapters. The things that I need for the flight (books, headphones, a small pillow, extra toiletries, travel documents, and money) are also in the computer bag.

Right: The Pelican Gustafson Safari Roller Case with zip-off computer bag. I use fitted neopreen bags for protecting the camera equipment. The bags are lighter and more compact than typical padded inserts.

My Packing List

Airline Tickets
Passport & Visa
Money (US + Kenya or Tanzania)
Toiletries—Razor, Brush, Tooth
Paste, Tooth Brush, Deodorant &
Shampoo
Clock (1) AAA,
Larium (Anti Malaria Pills)
Game Parks of East Africa Book
Journal & Pens
Bose Headphones (2)AAA
I POD & Charger
Eye Shade, Ear Plugs, Lip gloss,
Pillow
Vest
Flashlight (3) AAA
First Aid Kit
(2) Better Beamers
Bug spray
Suntan Lotion
Hat
Duct Tape
Clothes (7)
Socks (7)
Underwear (7)
Warm Shirt
(2) Long Sleeved, Light Shirts
(2) Short Sleeved, Light Shirts
Thermo shirt
(2) Long pants
(2) Shorts
TIP MONEY $20.00 per day per
person for your driver

D3, Charger, Extra Battery
D300, Charger, Extra Battery
Card Reader, Software
Lap Top, Mouse & Link Compact
Flash Cards
(4) 16 Gig & (4) 4 Gig
TODD-PLUG & UK Adapters
Battery Charger 110-220 Volts
AA Rechargeable Batteries (20)
AAA Rechargeable Batteries (8)
Camera & Flash Instruction
Books (PDF on Computer)
160 gig HYPERDRIVE® (Storage
Device)
Off Camera Flash Cord
SB800X Flash
Flash Arm & Wrench
Gitzo Tripod
Wimberly Tripod Head
Todd-Pod
17-35 mm Lens
35-70 mm Lens
80-200 mm Lens
200-400 mm Lens
600 mm Lens
1.4X Teleconverter
1.7 Teleconverter
2X Teleconverter
Camera Cleaning Kit:
Lens Pen, Micro Cloth, Lens
Cleaning Solution, Micro Tools
Under Plane 2 Cases—50 lbs
(each)
1 Carry-On Bag 22 lbs.

The items in red are packed in my carry on photo bag.
If my checked bags are lost or delayed I will still have everything
I need to photograph on safari.

Safari Tale #3

On the 2006 Tanzania Safari, one of the participants decided to pack his Nikon 600mm lens and D200 camera body in his checked bags. Unfortunately, upon arrival at Kilimanjaro International Airport, his bag was not on the carousel.

As is done with any bag that is missing, we reported it to the Lost Luggage Department. We were assured that the lost bag would be on the next flight from Amsterdam and would be delivered to our first game lodge in Tarangire National Park.

Annoying, but not the end of the world. He borrowed an extra camera and a 200-400mm lens from a kindhearted fellow photographer. That night at the lodge there was no sign of the bag, nor was there any sign of it on the following evening.

The next day we transferred to another game park, and still the luggage had not caught up with us. After two more days of anxious waiting, the luggage appeared, as if by magic, in his room. All of his camera equipment was there and intact! Throughout this ordeal, the photographer kept his perspective and his sense of humor. The loss of his luggage in no way affected the group's safari experience.

On the final day during our group's photo show and tell, he showed his favorite image of the whole safari, a photo of his complete set of luggage.

Lessons: *Carry what you need with you on the plane and keep a positive attitude at all times.*

On Safari

Keeping Your Photography Wits About You

The safari experience can be overwhelming due to jet-lag, culture shock, and unfamiliar vehicles. These distractions will be discussed in detail later in the book. Being unfamiliar with new equipment can be a huge challenge; it is amazing how many people buy new equipment, bring it to Africa, and have no idea how to use it. In the "heat of battle," when you are surrounded by the birds and animals that you came to photograph, don't forget the basics: use good sharpness techniques; check your histogram and check for flashing highlights; consider ISO, depth of field, and shutter speed; carefully select the AF points and the AF mode depending on the situation, and (I'm not kidding!) be sure to turn your camera on. The well-prepared photographer who knows his equipment and is confident in his skills will be at a great advantage in new and strange situations.

Many safari photographers get so excited when confronted by the multitude of subjects on safari that they lose all understanding of the things that are required to create a good image. You should be continually asking yourself: "Do I have a good light-angle to the subject? Is the subject in the clear with a clean background? Do I need flash?"

If you have a flash unit with you on safari, have it set up and on the camera with fresh batteries. If you have to go into your bag or back to your room to get the right equipment, you will undoubtedly miss the shot.

Subject Driven vs. Situation Driven Photography

A large part of a photographer's success is the choice of subjects. Shooting anything that moves and taking lots of frames does not guarantee high quality images. On an East African safari there are multitudes of subjects every day. The choice of which subjects to photograph directly affects the number of quality images captured on your safari.

Shooting a cheetah (Below left, Maasai Mara) in a poor setting, bad light, and in a static behavior just because it is a cheetah is what I refer to as "subject driven" photography. You can make powerful images of more mundane subjects, such as the White Pelican (Below right, Lake Naivasha), if they are in a good situation (good light, clean background, engaging behavior).

Safari Tale #4

With more than 450 bird species and countless photo opportunities, Lake Baringo is one of the premier bird photography locations in the world. In 1998, I brought Arthur Morris there for 3 days of our safari. It was so productive a location that after the first morning there, we changed the length of our stay to 6 days. I was photographing a White-bellied go away bird, using all the right techniques, including a low approach to create a soft, distant background. I had shot 3 rolls of this bird as it feasted on Aloe flowers when Art came up behind me and whispered "What are you photographing?" "A White-bellied go away bird," I answered. "The light is harsh; it will be a White-bellied throw away bird if you don't use your flash," he told me. I had my flash with me but had gotten carried away by the beauty of the subject and the great situation. I turned the flash on, set -1 stop of flash compensation, and made some beautiful pictures before the bird flew away. If I had needed to return to the room for the flash unit, I would have missed getting the images that I did. But though I had the flash in place, I still had to turn it on....

Lesson:

Have the equipment that you need with you and remember to use it.

White-bellied go away bird, Lake Baringo, Kenya

The end of a dusty safari drive, Ndudtu, Tanzania

Save Your Gear! Three Practical Considerations

The game drives you take on safari may be the most exciting photographic experiences of your life, as well as the most frustrating. These are three significant challenges you must face while on safari.

Dust

Unless it's raining, East African roads and safari tracks are dusty! Omnipresent dust is a detriment to the proper functioning of your camera equipment, mandating that you protect your equipment on game drives. Always keep the lower windows of your vehicle closed to prevent dust from blowing into the vehicle. Pro camera bodies are built tough, but require regular maintenance on safari.

1. Clean your equipment every day to prevent dust from working its way into critical areas of the body and lens. I use a large soft bristle artist's brush for dusting off camera and lens bodies when I return to the lodge. It works equally well with the computer key board. Warning: Cleaning with a damp cloth can turn the dust to mud. I don't bring compressed air since it doesn't travel well in the hold of the airplane. Simple but effective techniques often work best.

2. Clean your camera's sensor often. That speck of dirt or hair will be on every photo you take until it's cleaned. Learn how to lock up the mirror of your camera. The safest and quickest method I've found is the ®Lens Pen. As discussed previously, tap the head of the lens pen on a clean cloth to remove the graphite from the tip. Once your camera's mirror is locked up, it's simple to wipe the pen gently across the sensor and remove all the dust.

Dry mud cracks, Ngorongoro Crater, Tanzania

3. Don't forget the front element/filter of your camera lens. Be assured, it will have a coating of dust. The longer you wait to clean it, the less accurate your focus tracing will be, the more images you will miss and the more frustrated you will become. I always carry (and USE) a bottle of lens cleaning solution and a large micro fiber cloth on every game drive.

Please do not panic about the dust to the detriment of your safari photography. Some folks have gone to extremes to protect their equipment by keeping cameras in zip lock plastic bags at all times, missing scores of good photographic situations because it was too time consuming to unpack the cameras.

Another strategy is to cover the front of telephoto lenses with hotel shower caps. The elastic trimmed caps fit nicely over the lens hood and keep most of the safari dust off the front element. Too often, when a subject is approached, the crinkly sound of removing the shower cap from the lens frightens the subject. When you are traveling with your equipment on the roof of the vehicle, try to keep the front of your lens pointed backward to prevent it from looking like a dusty, bug-spattered windshield.

Bumpy Roads

Game park road circuits can be rough. Ruts, stones, and washboard sections can be bone jarring, much less equipment jarring. I find that on a game drive it is much easier to stand while the vehicle is moving. First of all, you are using your legs as shock absorbers. Secondly, and more importantly, you will also be in position to photograph BEFORE the vehicle stops. The roads between towns, cities and game parks can be just as rough and the problem is magnified by the vehicle's speed. Some photographers try to save time by editing images and backing up files on their computer during road trips between park destinations. Warning: Computers have lots of little moving parts that are critical to their operation. Jarring bumps on rough roads can throw moving parts out of whack, causing a computer to crash. Keep your computer turned off when travelling.

Rain

I am often asked when I go on safari "Is it winter there or summer?" At the equator, there isn't a winter or summer. In Tanzania and Kenya, it is either the rainy season or the dry season. The short rains are around November and December. There is a period of dry weather (or less rain) from January to early March. Long rains tend to be from April to June. The longer dry season lasts from July to October.

These seasons are wildly variable. Some years there are no short rains and other years may see the short rains continue into the long rains without break. To compli-

A fallen fig tree and rough safari track, Lake Manyara, Tanzania

cate matters further, different regions within East Africa have variations of the dry season/rainy season cycle. For example, Tanzania's Tarangire National park may get no rain during the weeks where the southern Serengeti experiences torrential rains. To further complicate matters, it is very difficult to know, with any certainty, what the weather will be like on a given safari. In the last decade, regional trends in climate have produced longer dry spells than usual and some regions have experienced severe droughts. The last few years in Amboseli, however, have produced heavier rains making the marshes spectacular areas for birds and elephants.

Squal, Maasai Mara, Kenya

Cheetah in the rain, Ndudtu, Tanzania

Because of the wide variability of the seasons in East Africa, your safari dates may coincide with the onset of the rains. That doesn't mean your photo safari is doomed. Often, the rains only last for part of the day, allowing for regular game drives and "dry photography." If there are long periods of rain, you can still find passable roads to travel in the parks, as well as opportunities around the lodges. Spectacular images can still be made in the middle of a torrential downpour. In heavy rain, your driver will undoubtedly close the roof hatches to protect the vehicle. When this happens, you will be able to shoot out the windows of the vehicle, using your camera bag as a platform on which to rest your camera rig.

I pack a large garbage bag in my camera bag and have an umbrella handy for cloud bursts. The umbrella can be duct taped to the tripod if there are long periods of rain. If you are hiking, the garbage bag can protect your entire rig. When it's dry, you've already learned about DUST.

The Vehicle's the Variable: Your Photo Platform

Know Your Safari Vehicle

Most photographs made on safari in East Africa are created either from a Safari Van or a 4-wheel drive vehicle. When choosing a land operator, one of the primary considerations should be the type of vehicle the company will use. In addition, consider the reliability of the vehicle, its upkeep, the seating capacity, and most important of all, the hatch configuration. I travel only in vehicles with three open roof hatches.

I organize my photo safaris under the assumption that there will be no more than three photographers per 8-passenger vehicle so that each photographer has a full set of seats (window to window) for themselves. With only three folks per vehicle, there is plenty of seat room for photographic equipment. And best of all, each person has their own roof hatch for photography.

Safari Vans

Safari vans are passenger vans that have been modified with heavy duty seats and open roof hatches. (I do not use safari vans on my trips.) When compared to the four wheel drive Land Rovers, they offer an affordable alternative. The vans are comfortable and ride fairly smoothly, but they do not have off-road capabilities. In game parks and reserves where off-road driving is allowed vans have to stay on the road. These vehicles have short life expectancies due to the rough driving conditions. High-end safari companies replace their van fleet every two years. The old vans often are sold to smaller (and less expensive) safari operators. If the operator you're considering uses safari vans, then you should carefully weigh the factors mentioned above.

Some vans have a single, large roof hatch. Sometimes these single hatches do not provide equal access for all of the photographers. The front passenger may have to lean back and the back photographer may have to hunch forward to access the opening. These models will most always have a permanent pop-up hatch cover designed to shade the van's occupants. This type of roof hatch is problematic from several reasons:

1. The single hatch opening only has 4 corners on which all photographers can set camera supports. The person in the front has the two front corners, and the person in the rear has the two back corners. The photographer in the middle is just out of luck. This situation obviously causes problems.

2. When raised to their fixed positions, the permanent pop-up hatch covers are high enough to clear the heads of anyone 5'8" or shorter. Anyone taller than that will eventually smash their heads so many times they might consider leaving the vehicle! This option would clearly make photographing lion kills more exciting...

3. The hatch cover is mounted on permanent bars. These supports are placed right in the corners of the hatch—the ideal spots to place your camera equipment...

4. In these types of vehicles it is impossible to use the Todd-Pod/Wimberley head combination.

If you do opt to travel in a safari van due to financial considerations, I suggest that you contact your safari vendor to make sure that the van you use will have three hatches.

A safari vehicle in trouble, Ngorongoro Crater

Four Wheel Drive Vehicles

Four-wheel drive vehicles are my favorites for safari. Their long wheelbases and four-wheel drive capabilities allow them to be driven off road through a trackless savannah, to negotiate rocky terrain, or ford shallow streams. For decades, Land Rover Defenders were the vehicle of choice to handle the rough roads and formidable off-road driving conditions encountered on safari drives. The reliability of these vehicles has been in question, but drivers have become expert at repairing them in the field and carry spare parts for the most common breakdowns.

The problem of the Land Rovers' squeaking brakes has plagued me for years. There is a design flaw in these brakes that allows road dust to build up on the break drums; causing a high-pitched, ear-splitting squeal. The squealing always seems to get louder as you approach a beautiful, rare, shy subject in great light in a wonderful situation. In these cases, the animals head for the hills, not because they are frightened, but because they are annoyed.

The Toyota Range Rover is newer to the safari scene and is more reliable and quieter than the Land Rover. The best bet is to find a company whose vehicles have three open roof-hatches with fully removable hatch covers.

Always Help Pull Them Out!

When you come across a vehicle stuck inn the mud, should your drivers stop and help? Yes. It may be you tomorrow. Any driver or car can get stuck. If you see someone who needs help, please encourage your driver to provide assistance. Some safari groups seem to think their time as more important than anyone else's, but I'm sure they would want help, if they were the ones who were stuck!

Safari Photo Techniques
Photographing From a Vehicle

All of the photographs in this section were made from four-wheel drive vehicles on game drives in Tanzania and Kenya

You have taken great pains to get your essential photo equipment to Africa, so it only makes sense to have it within easy reach when you need it. Whether you use a rolling bag, an over-the-shoulder bag, or a photo backpack, you will need to re-pack for game drive photography when you arrive. With three photographers per vehicle, there will plenty of room for your equipment.

My big lens with my main camera body attached and turned on (always mounted on the Wimberley head and Todd-Pod), are on top of the vehicle so that I am ready to photograph at all times. I like to have my bag on one of the seats in my row with the extra gear. My second camera body is on the other seat with a mid-sized telephoto lens (often a zoom lens) mounted on it. My teleconverters are in my vest pockets,

This view of an African safari track illustrates the importance of having a good qualit... safari vehicle. I can't remember if we took the left or the right track but I do remember tha... we got through in the Toyota 4-wheel drive vehicle.

Safari Tale #5

Ndutu, in the Tanzania's Ngorongoro Conservation Area, is located at the southern end of Olduvai Gorge. There is a chain of small lakes that are the hub of the marsh ecosystem. The marsh is a great place to photograph any number of animals.

For famed bird photographer Arthur Morris, the main attraction of the marsh was the abundance of beautiful shorebirds. Sandpipers, plovers, avocets, and stilts are common in the small pools on the edges of the marsh. One of the many elements that make Arthur's photographs so dynamic and stunningly beautiful is his total awareness of light angle. On safari, he is constantly directs the driver to the very best light angle: "Pull forward 2 feet. Back up 3 feet. Forward 6 inches".

Arthur spotted a three-banded plover wading in a pool next to a small spit of land. He had the driver move the Land Rover onto the spit for a better light angle. (He likes his shadow to point directly at the subject.)

When the bird moved to the far edge of the pool, Art told the driver to re-position the van. Things were still not quite perfect, so Art said "Hard left and forward one meter." The van was in perfect position and level as could be. As the three photographers began to photograph they felt a strange sensation as the edge of the spit beneath the front and rear left tires collapsed and the left side of the Land Rover sank deeply into the marsh.

To this day, whenever Art is on the scene, our veteran drivers ask (very politely) "Hard left?"

Lesson: No vehicle, driver, or photographer is infallible.... and sometimes the picture isn't as good as the story.

and my extra CF cards are in an easily accessible pocket. My flash is either mounted to the flash arm or in the camera bag (where it is ready to be attached at a moment's notice). There are times when the roads are simply too rough to keep the flash mounted. The bouncing and pounding can be rough on the weakest point of the system: the hot-shoe of the flash. The newer Nikon flashes have a metal shoe, but I still take the flash off when the roads are rough. By getting in the habit of storing your equipment in the same place, you will be able to find it quickly.

There are many strategies for photographing from safari vehicles. I use my 600mm lens 95% of the time. Whether I am using the big lens with teleconverters or using the straight 600, my rig is always mounted on the Wimberley Head atop a Todd-Pod. This set-up fits perfectly on the corner of the roof hatches with the feet over the rim of the hatch to hold it in place. When the vehicle is in motion, I am always standing with my head and shoulders out of the roof hatch on the lookout for good subjects. I place a forearm over the Todd-Pod and hold onto the roll bar above the rim of the roof hatches. By doing this, I am able to keep the rig in place even on the roughest roads.

Approaching a Subject & Positioning the Van

Most often, the drivers try to help by getting you as close to the subject as is safely possible. With super-telephotos "as close as possible" is often too close. Early in the safari, while talking to your driver about van positioning, it is a good idea to have your driver look through your long lens. Give him an idea of what you will be seeing. Your driver's familiarity with long lens photography will improve the odds that each approach you make to the subject will go just as you want it to.

Once the vehicle is stopped, it is of vital importance that everyone is ready to shoot. Standing while the vehicle is in motion, with your equipment in place on the roof hatch makes this possible. As stated earlier, the safest and most efficient way I've found to travel with the big lens on top is to have my equipment mounted to a Todd-Pod. This rests on the frame of the roof hatch and is safely held in place by my supporting arm as I firmly hold the vehicle's roll bar.

Some people opt to sit while the vehicle is in motion and during the approach. They do not realize that when they stand up to get their gear in place they will almost always rock the van to the point that no one can make sharp images. This important issue should be discussed early on in the safari so that critical photo opportunities are not lost and people's feelings don't get hurt. In many photo situations there is a very narrow window of time in which to photograph the subject that you so painstakingly approached.

Others may be physically unable to stand for a full safari game drive. Those who choose to sit during the approaches might best be discouraged from standing up until everyone else has made a few photographs. Many grazing antelopes will look at you when the vehicle stops for just a single second before they turn tail and flee. In this case, you may get a second chance to photograph when the animal reaches

Using a Todd-Pod

The Todd-Pod can be used with a Wimberley mount or a ball head to photograph from the roof of the safari vehicle. With the camera always set up on the Todd-Pod in the corner of the hatch, I hold the vehicle's roll bar and keep my forearm pressed down on the tongue of the Todd-Pod. This way I keep myself stable and my camera system secure, and I am ready to shoot at a moment's notice.

The next step in the process is reading the direction of the light. I always keep the Todd-Pod set up on the side from which I plan to shoot. For example, if the sun is on the left side of the vehicle and the most direct light angle is on the right side, it only makes sense to have the Todd-Pod set up on the right side and look for subjects on that side.

Safari tracks tend to meander and as a result the light angle will change from one side of the van to the other. I am constantly aware of this and change the position of the Todd-Pod accordingly. If your rig is set up on the wrong side of the vehicle as a shy subject is approached, you will likely miss the shot. It is likely that you will shake the van while you are moving your rig from one side to the other and the motion alone is often enough to flush a wary bird. On the other hand, even the shyest of birds will often stay for at least one shutter release if the photographer is prepared to shoot the instant the van stops.

This may seem like shameless promotion, but the reality is that the Todd-Pod was designed and built to make creating better quality photos easier.

Eye level view of an approaching male lion, Maasai Mara, Kenya

An Approach and the Final Image

This photograph of a caramel-colored black-maned lion was made possible by utilizing seven of the strategies that were discussed in previous sections. The first involved sighting the subject. Our van was one of a group of vehicles watching a family of cheetahs in a boulder-strewn area. We had the sun backlighting the cheetahs. Knowing that there were prides of lions in the area, I asked our driver if he thought they might come out to hunt. He thought that the cheetah mother would keep the cubs in the rocks for safety. With that in mind, we began looking for a lion or two while the other vans stayed with the cheetah family.

Our driver wanted to try a new area where there were no other vehicles. As we drove across the grassy ridges of the Maasai Mara, Euticus said, "I have seen him." I knew from the tone of his voice that it would be something good. A huge, solitary male lion was walking through the golden, head-high grass. Our approach totaled about three kilometers. When we saw the animal we discussed the ultimate photo. Our goal was to be directly in front of the lion as he approached us through the grass. The challenges were an approach over rough ground, the tall grass, and a moving subject.

Even with things seeming to work to perfection—the animal was in the clear, facing us, the van was in great position, and everyone had a clear shot—other factors affected the final image. In this case the problem was, as it often is with big male lions, that the subject had it's eyes closed; they often look like they are sleep-walking. On this magnificent animal's first pass, everyone in the van was thrilled with the approach and with the image that they had created. Then I asked them to look closely at their images while paying special attention to the subject's eyes; in every single image the lion's eyes were closed. We made another wide circular approach and stopped half a kilometer ahead of the lion in hopes of getting a second opportunity. In the final image, the eyes are open, the animal is in the clear, and the lower perspective attained by photographing from the opened side window angle allowed the softly-focused grasses to surround the subject.

its "safe zone" where it may pose briefly before beginning to graze again. Once the grazing behavior resumes, it is time to find a new subject. Don't waste time waiting for them to look at you again. They know you are there and they are not interested in you. Banging on the roof, whistling and clapping your hands are all annoying and can frighten the animals.

Perfect van placement, Ndutu, Tanzania

I encourage safari members to choose a van leader for each game drive, one per vehicle. The van leader is responsible for communicating with the driver as to van placement. All too often, the van leader tries to give instructions to the driver with his head and shoulders out of the van and the driver 4 feet away on the other side of the ceiling of the Land Rover. A Land Rover driving over a trackless savannah is a noisy contraption at best, so the situation described above assures that the driver will hear only a smattering of the instructions. In addition, a noisy approach often causes the animal to run away. When a bird flies or an animal heads for the bush, the resulting frustration is often focused on the driver.

If you are the van leader, here is how it should be done: When you spot a desirable subject, stop a good distance from the ultimate location. Tell the folks in your van of the plan so that everyone can envision the image that they wish to create and can choose the right focal length. Be sure to let them know which side of the van you will be photographing from and whether they should place their rigs on the front of their hatch or the rear.

Bend forward so that the driver can hear you clearly and explain the ideal approach to him. If possible, describe a curved path rather than a direct line. Let your driver know how you would like the van angled once you reach the best spot. Many drivers will stop the vehicle so that it is parallel the road, the track, or the subject. This often works well for game viewing, but not for photographers; having to twist your body results in an uncomfortable shooting stance. A much better strategy is to angle the van 45 degrees to the subject with each photographer's rig placed in the appropriate corner of the roof hatch. Everyone will have a good angle to the subject and a comfortable stance.

This ideal scenario is not always possible. There may be rocky ground, water, mud, or brush along your chosen approach. Here is where teamwork between the van leader and the driver can make or break the shooting situation. The best technique is for the van leader to bend so that his head is just inside the roof hatch, eyes just above the roof, mouth just below it, not far from the driver's ear. In this manner, the van leader can give final approach instructions to the driver in a normal voice while keeping his eyes on the subject.

"Hard right...soft left...straight on to that bush...hard left in front of the bush...50 meters straight ahead... pole, pole (slow), or haraka, haraka (fast)...20 meters...10 meters...simama (stop). I am still standing in the vehicle with my hand holding the vehicle's roll bar and camera. When the van stops, I am ready to shoot. Often, a situation will present itself that requires a fast stop and quick reflexes to make an image almost instantly. Whether the subject is a beautiful bird on a perfect perch, or a pair of battling zebras, you may never see anything like it again. **It is crucial that you are ready to shoot at a moment's notice.**

The #1 Cause of Missed Photo Opportunities on safari is that the vast majority of photographers are not prepared to begin photographing the moment the van stops. I have mentioned this previously, but it is so significant to your success that I want to clarify and reinforce the principle.

From reading this guide, you already know that road conditions are less than ideal on a game drive. Standing in the open hatch while the vehicle is moving is tiring and will at times leave you a bit bruised, so some people prefer to sit. If, however, your primary goal is capture peak action and dramatic animal and bird portraits on your safari, it is mandatory that you stand in the vehicle with your gear in place as it is approaching the subject. You don't have time to stand up, reach for your camera rig on the seat beside you, and locate the subject. And the same goes for aiming, framing, focusing, and coming up with the right exposure. The vehicle is your photo platform, and its stability is directly related to the quality of the images made by all. Anyone who is moving about to collect gear after the vehicle stops is creating vibrations that will make it impossible for others in the van to create sharp images. It is also important to note that talking in the vehicle during the final approach is likely to scare away wild animals and birds. Work with your vehicle-mates to develop strategies that ensure that the photographic opportunities will be maximized.

Working With Your Driver

While traveling abroad, I believe it is important to realize that you are a visitor in a foreign country. Be sure to treat all local people with respect. This is of utmost importance to the process of having an enjoyable and rewarding photo safari. The person you will have the most contact with will be your safari driver/guide. He is the one who will have the greatest influence over the safety and comfort of your safari experience, so treat him with the most respect.

Falling into his job description are such responsibilities as handling vouchers for hotels and game parks, driving you safely to and from your destinations, maintaining the safari vehicles in the roughest of driving conditions, and having a ready knowledge of the birds, animals, and habitats that you will be photographing. Safari drivers have a great deal of experience in knowing the habits of the animals and where they are likely to be found. Each driver has been certified after completing a rigorous training regimen.

Drivers, however, are not usually photography experts. They will spot subjects and get you close to them, but they are not mind readers. When the driver has trouble correctly positioning the vehicle, clients can get frustrated. Often the problem is caused by the photographer's lack of skill in directing the driver or his inability to communicate effectively with the driver.

Safari drivers are educated, highly trained professional naturalists. At times, I have observed a client treating a driver in a condescending manner. Cultural and language differences between a client and a driver are often the cause, but there is simply no excuse for such behavior. If you alienate your driver, you are jeopardizing the success of the entire safari.

A traveler's lack of cultural awareness can cause misunderstandings as to how or when things should happen. The traveler's logical plan for the day may have nothing to do with what is safe, expedient, or even legal. The drivers rely on years of experience when making decisions. If a van-mate's treatment of a driver is poor or boorish, your intercession on the driver's behalf will enhance your relationship with the driver. Rely on your driver's knowledge of game park boundaries and rules and the permit laws that govern safari vehicles. Game parks, game reserves, and conservation areas have boundaries that are not always readily apparent to the visiting photographer.

Trust your guide completely. Rely on his experience. He will always make informed decisions as to where you can go and when you can go there. It validates his purpose as an integral part of the safari team. Feel free to ask questions about where you are going and why, but never argue or beg once he has answered. Keeping everyone involved in the planning will result in a more successful safari. Please do not pressure your driver to ignore park rules so that you can get the photograph that you want. Oftentimes breaking game park rules results in not only a fine, but in the loss of the driver's Guide Papers and his ability to make a living as a safari driver.

Safari Tale #6

As we entered a marshy area in Maasai Mara National Reserve, a small black bird scurried across the Nile-cabbage-covered pool. My thought was "African crake," an extremely shy bird that I had seen previously only from a distance. While it is common to see African jacana, moorhens, and Lily trotters, this bird was much smaller and ran much faster than any of those species. The situation seemed worth investigating so we stopped the van immediately and I devised a plan. "Let's drive along the marsh with the reeds on our right. When we get to the break in the reeds, be ready to photograph from the right side of the vehicle. Start focusing as the vehicle stops. By the time the van stops, we should have about a second and a half before the crake disappears." And that is exactly what happened. When we got to the break in the reeds, the crake was just coming into the clear. I began focusing as soon as I could see the bird. The auto-focus locked onto the subject just as the ve-hicle stopped moving. I made two images before the bird ran into the reeds. It was all over in a heartbeat.

Lesson:

Keep your eyes peeled for the unexpected and be ready to act quickly. Study and learn the habits and behaviors of potential subjects.

Black Crake, Maasai Mara, Kenya

Get to know your driver early in the safari. Ask him about his family, his home. Find out what his favorite game park is, his favorite bird or animal. Let him know what you are especially interested in photographing; he will do everything in his power to find it for you.

Ask your driver for advice. Rely on his training and experience. He will let you know what the best options are. The parks are divided into circuits that define the scope of a safari drive. Clients often want to see the whole park in one game drive. My advice is to let your driver show you the park on his time table. He knows the habits and habitats of specific birds and animal species and knows when and where they might best be found. There are specialties in each park that are most easily photographed at specific times of day. Your driver will also have talked to the other drivers at the lodge and on the road and will have an excellent idea of what is possible for your game drive.

Teamwork Promotes Success

Which group would find the most photographic opportunities, a van with a single photographer or a van with three cooperative photographers? Would two sets of eyes likely "see" as many opportunities as four?

Respect and Communication

Knowing a few words in Swahili will show your driver, as well as others with whom you are working, that you are making an effort at understanding his world. You will soon find out if your accent is registering with him as intelligible language. They may understand your English better than your Swahili. Either way, you have made the effort. Here are a few Swahili words that you might wish to learn:

Let's go	*twende*
Stop	*simama*
Straight ahead	*moja kwa moja*
Slowly	*pole pole*
Go left	*kwa kushoto*
Go right	*kwa kulia*
Please	*tafadhali*
Thank you	*asante*

I have only had one driver who did not respond well to the words and phrase above. I would give clear instructions to him to turn left and he would turn right. I would say right and he would turn left. Once I discovered that he was practically deaf, it was easy to get a handle on the situation. We then used hand signals and a touch on the shoulder to communicate effectively for the rest of the safari.

Lesson: *You will benefit from effective communication with your driver.*

It is a given that everyone in the safari vehicle wishes to make the best photographs that his or her equipment and skill will allow. Communicating well with others in your van and understanding their needs will create a mood of cooperation that will lead to better photographs for everyone involved.

Each time the vehicle is stopped, it is up to the van leader to make sure that everyone has as clear a shot. He should do his best to make sure that there are no branches blocking the subject and that everyone has a clean background.

Safari Tale #7

There is an issue of American slang vs. the English language. Unless you communicate clearly, the way you tell the driver where to place the van may not make sense to your driver. I realized this early in my safari career when we were in position to photograph a beautiful leopard at Kenya's Lake Nakuru National Park. The driver had positioned the van so that distracting branches were no longer in the photo area. As the cat stretched and yawned, it moved a few feet down the branch to a point where obstructing branches again became an issue. I told the driver to "move up". He looked at the branch containing the leopard, then looked back at me with a confused look and said "Up there?"

"Move up" meant something very different to my driver than it did to me.

Lesson: *Speak plainly when giving directions. If there seems to be confusion, talk to your driver and see what works for both of you.*

Leopard, Lake Nakuru, Kenya

Sometimes this is not possible and someone in the van will have an obstructed view. When this happens, those with a clear view will need to make a few images quickly. Then the van needs to be repositioned as quickly as possible. Hopefully, the subject will not have moved in that time. Good teamwork will build trust as people look out for their fellow photographers and not just themselves.

When a photographic situation nears its end, it's natural to think about finding something else to shoot. Those who are done photographing will begin to move equipment. This movement causes the van to rock while others in the van may still be photographing. It is, therefore, good form to quietly ask if everyone is done shooting. If anyone is still shooting, everyone else should keep still until they are done. Everyone needs to secure their equipment before the van starts to roll. The van leader should make sure to get an "OK" from everyone before he tells the driver to start moving the van.

Impatience

Impatience can cause tension that will detract from the quality of a safari. For those on their first safari, it is hard to resist the urge to want to create an entire East African portfolio in just a single day. Everything is brand new and they have not seen or photographed any of it before.

Common Pressures Placed on Drivers

- To enter the park earlier or depart later than park rules allow.

- To leave the road or track to get closer to that Cape buffalo.

- To cross a park boundary to get closer to that sleeping leopard.

- To drive over to that group of vans following the hunting cheetahs.

- To rush across the park to see the rhino the other vans found.

- To let me get out of the van to get a better shot.

- To beep the horn to get that bird to fly.

- To move closer to the foraging elephant to get it to turn around.

- To drive across a stream instead of driving around it.

- To stay by the cheetah cubs for the rest of the morning to see what they do.

- Find a leopard now!

Titus Musimba with ostrich eggs, Maasai Mara, Kenya

Euticus Muragi, Lake Nakuru, Kenya

This is one of my favorite safari driver photos. In this situation we were surrounded by a pride of lions in Ndutu. Salvatore, the driver in the van next to us, was unaware of the approaching lioness. From another vehicle I had a good angle to shoot through his window at f22 to add enough depth of field to make this an effective photo.

They have put a lot of time, effort and money into their photographic safari. When either of you miss a chance to create a great image, the frustration can be intense. Having patience and realizing that each day of the safari will yield more chances to capture great images can help alleviate the frustration.

I have the philosophy of letting the safari come to me. I don't get as much enjoyment or as great a return of quality images when I "chase" the safari. "Chasing" means driving as fast as possible to get from one subject to the next and panicking if there isn't a new subject right around the next bush. With nothing to photograph the tendency is to drive faster to find new subjects. If a subject is found, some will move the van numerous times to get to the "right" spot for the photograph. I think a good strategy is to pick out where the best spot might be from a distance and go there the first time. If your subject is active, wait in your chosen spot to see if they will create a powerful scene for you as they move around. If you have the vehicle do the moving, the chances are the subject will have moved from the ultimate position by the time you reposition the vehicle. By using this strategy, I am likely to average 30 high quality images per day while on safari.

Competitiveness

Competitiveness often rears it ugly head on photographic safaris. On my group safaris, we almost always have multiple vans, but we do not travel in convoy. If one van does follow the other, the second van may or may not have a chance with the same subject and the third van will usually have no chance at all. The vans behind the first one usually wind up eating lots of dust.

When my vehicles leave the lodge compound, they branch out onto different tracks. More ground is covered that way. Each group of photographers finds their own subjects and makes their own images. It is easy to come back from a game drive excited about the shots of the day. Someone in another van may have seen that cheetah that you so desperately wanted to photograph. Instead of getting angry with them because you didn't see it, be happy for them. There will be times that you see something that no one else sees. You would want people to be happy for your good fortune. The law of averages works here. Everyone will get some great opportunities and everyone will miss some great opportunities.

The vans are equipped with radios and all the drivers carry cell phones so there is communication between the vans. If one of the vehicles finds a leopard or a cheetah family with cubs, the drivers will share the information and you will be able to drive to that location. You should not expect a call if a van is photographing a martial eagle in a tree or elephants jousting. These events are fleeting. If a vehicle leaves an existing photographic situation in an attempt to get to the jousting elephants, the behavior will undoubtedly be over before they arrive. This will of course cause even more frustration.

Lion cub, Ndutu, Tanzania

Safari Tale #8

We had spent the morning searching unsuccessfully for a leopard. Our driver suggested that we explore a different part of the park that afternoon; he had heard of a pride of lions there, with cubs. As you can see, his suggestion was excellent. Instead of continuing to hunt fruitlessly for a leopard, we spent an enjoyable afternoon watching and photographing these playful cats.

Lesson: *Listen to the expert.*

Photographing from a Vehicle Window

Images taken from the top of a safari van can have a look of sameness to them. Try opening the lower window of the vehicle for a different perspective; the resulting images are often more dramatic, and photographing from the subject's eye level often yields a more intimate feel to an image. I keep a second camera body with a midrange telephoto lens (usually the Nikon f/4 200-400mm) on one of the window seats. I often use this lens when photographing out of an open window, but I sometimes move the 600mm lens from the roof down to the side window. Remember, if you drive with the side windows open, dust will be sucked into the vehicle. Protect your camera gear and make it easier for everyone to breathe by opening the side windows only when an appropriate situation develops and by shutting them when you are done.

These images of a zebra colt illustrate two distinctly different views. The top image was taken from the roof of a safari vehicle. Notice that even with the 600mm lens at a wide open aperture (f/4), the background is somewhat distracting. Without moving the van or changing my camera settings I created the image below from the side window.

Here are some of the things that I considered:

1. There was nothing of a distracting nature behind the colt (trees, bushes, shadows, or other animals).

2. Knowing that the zebra colts can be shy and nervous, I lowered the window well in advance of the final approach and positioning of the vehicle; the last thing that I wanted was for this colt to run and hide behind his mother for protection.

3. I created a few images from the top of the van while the young zebra's head was down to illustrate these points. After letting my van mates know my intentions ahead of time, I moved my camera gear to the lower window in super-slow motion so that my movement would not negatively affect their efforts.

Different angles of view of a zebra colt, Ngorongoro Crater, Tanzania

Time Management

Your punctuality and your attitude about being on time will directly affect the other people in your group (and vice-versa). On the first day of a safari the leaders need to let folks know that they are depending on everyone to be on time every day. Period! There are certain hours of the day when the animals and birds are most active and most easily photographed, and these hours generally offer the most beautiful lighting conditions as well.

Safari time is precious. Photographable predawn activity begins at about 6:30 AM. People should not be loading up the vans at 6:30. At 6:30 the van should be out of the gate and into the park searching for subjects. To facilitate a prompt departure, have a discussion with your safari group about early departures. It may be that some would prefer to stay in bed if the hour is too early. Be sure to let the group know the night before if you do not intend to take the morning game drive. Sometimes skipping a single game drive can provide much-needed rest. A safari can be a grueling experience and being overly tired will lower both your creativity and your photographic productivity.

To this point, the discussion of photographic subjects has mostly centered on large mammals. In reality, much of your safari time might well be spent photographing birds. There is a difference between photographing birds and bird watching. I get nervous when people tell the driver to stop so that they can get the binoculars out to see a distant bird. The seemingly innocent act of stopping, getting out the field glasses, and discussing species possibilities nearly always results in the driver getting out the bird guide book... The wait can be interminable for serious photographers. If you are on a photographic safari, this is not a wise use of time.

Over the course of a safari, hours can be lost viewing far away little birds, hours that could have been spent more wisely photographing appropriate subjects. Birders enjoy identifying birds and checking them off the list, but this has little or nothing to do with bird photography. A bird photographer will enjoy a bird 25 feet away, in beautiful light, on a nice perch, with a clear background and not care what kind of bird it is. For those who are interested in birding, many lodges have such opportunities around the lodge grounds. All tour leaders and organizers should make it clear to potential clients that theirs is a serious Photo-Safari and that folks interested in birding should join a safari that more closely suits their needs.

Sleeping lions, Ngorongoro Crater, Tanzania

The Sleeping Lion Syndrome

Lions are on everyone's "must see and photograph" list. Until a safari group finds their first lion, there will be a sense of anticipation that grows with each passing day. When that first lion is spotted, there is a buzz of excitement in the safari group. The lions' mystique ensures them a place among the "Big Five." They are huge, beautiful cats at the top of the food chain. They can be dramatic, humorous, or powerful. What most first time safari participants don't understand is that lions sleep during 80% of the daylight hours. If the lion that you find is asleep, the chances are that it will remain asleep.

On a typical safari, you may well see as many as 60 lions. Passing on the opportunity to watch lions sleep in the hot sun will significantly increase your chances of seeing other lions (or other subjects) that are awake and active.

Remember, while you are watching a sleeping lion, somewhere else, there may be other animals that are eating, being eaten, drinking, mating, fighting, playing, giving birth, or being born. Safari time is precious!

Species Overkill

As your safari evolves, you will undoubtedly have seen and photographed such common animals as impala, giraffe, zebra, and elephant. As you check these species off your "Record Shot " list, here are two things to think about.

1. Once you have successfully photographed a species, you don't need to take any more portraits of that species (unless you find the animal in gorgeous light in a gorgeous setting). This will allow you the freedom to search for new and different subjects. Some people do not get to this stage until late in the safari. They feel the need to photograph anything that moves. This may be due to inexperience or to the fact that they paid for an expensive safari and want to get all the images that they can. In reality, they will get fewer great shots because they are satisfied by pursuing subjects they have already photographed.

2. It is, however, extremely important to recognize interesting species behavior. Your group may have plenty of Thompson's gazelle photographs and may not be the least bit interested in stopping for "another Thompson's gazelle." Nonetheless, if you are aware of animal behavior characteristics, you will recognize the opportunity to capture additional dramatic behavior.

For example, while on a game drive you notice that there are several male Thompson's gazelles on the edge of a breeding herd and they are displaying aggressive behavior. A full scale jousting match breaks out between the dominant male and an interloper. You are able to photograph this event because you were paying attention to the subject's behavior, rather than just the species alone. Be aware of these situations with any animal group you pass. You can capture amazing images of subjects you might have thought you had fully covered...

The photos on the right illustrate the importance of knowing your subjects and their behaviors. The first image is of a black-shouldered kite in a nice situation. The conversation that accompanied that morning's photo shoot at Lake Manyara National Park was: "Got it. OK, let's go... Wait a second. When we move the van, he may squawk at us because we are right on the edge of his circle of fear." By knowing the bird's probable reaction to our movement we were able to create something more than static portraits of this beautiful bird.

The bird in the third image was spotted a half hour later perched quite a distance away. "We already have a black-shouldered kite. Let's keep going." Instead of moving on, we took time to look through our long lenses and quickly realized that this bird did not have black shoulders; it was a pallid harrier, a species that we had not yet photographed.

Black-shouldered kite and display, Lake Manyara, Tanzania

Pallid harrier and display, Lake Manyara, Tanzania

Surrounded lion, Ngorongoro Crater, Tanzania

Safari Tale #9

It can be tempting to join a "Safari Traffic Jam." This photo illustrates a classic example of what to avoid on a safari drive. Lions are on everyone's "most wanted" list as soon as they begin planning a safari. As a photographer, my most wanted subjects are those in great photographic situations. This lion had been crossing the Ngorongoro Crater floor on the way back to the pride. I did not like the fact that a throng of safari

vehicles had chased it, surrounded it, and eventually blocked its way. What I did like about the situation was: With all the vans massed in one place, our photo group would have the rest of the Crater to ourselves!

Lesson: *Safari time is precious. Choose your subjects with care.*

Develop Your Photographic View

In this critical section, I want to share how I have sought to develop my photographic vision, view, style, and craft. Prior to each safari, I consider what I have accomplished previously and attempt to clarify my goals for the upcoming trip. Besides the obvious internal contemplation this entails, I have also asked people who are familiar with my work and style what new vision they thought I might develop on the upcoming safari. Some of my early safaris were especially portrait-heavy. I have heard some photographers discount portraiture. "That's already been done!" they say. I have always said "If you haven't done it, give it a try." Shoot subjects that are interesting to you as portraiture. If you don't already have the portrait, why not take it? Having a super telephoto that allows for intimate portraits provides one means of accomplishing this. As an added benefit, I make lots of sales of simple animal and bird portraiture.

On one safari, I used high f stops and slow shutter speeds to create long-exposure blurs. On another trip, I focused on capturing images that illustrated the constant action found in nature. Beyond photographing the peak of the action, there are other important elements in a sequence of images that can help to tell the complete story. Later safaris allowed for the challenge of finding subjects groups, providing thematic patterns of doubles and triples. I concentrated on creating mirror-like images of animals and birds and photographs of interacting pairs. Still another theme involved making images with the front subject in sharp focus and with a second similar subject behind the first in soft focus. It is amazing what possibilities you can come up with when you learn to think outside of the box. These stylistic and technique-driven considerations are the reason why photographers "in the know" look beyond shooting a list of animal portraits on safari. Photographers with good creative vision will employ a variety of styles and techniques, and they will invariably end up with interesting and dynamic portfolios.

Sparring Thompson gazelles, Lake Nakuru, Kenya

These photographers use different lenses and artistic views to capture the same subject.

The following pages contain images that illustrate how the technical decisions that you make and the techniques that you use will affect the images that you create. Issues dealing with focal length choices, shutter speeds, ISO settings, depth-of-field, and framing (among many others) will have to be dealt with each time the vehicle prepares to stop. For you to be successful, these artistic and technical decisions will have to be made in advance so that you will be ready to act as soon as the safari vehicle is in position.

Black and white colobus, Elsemere, Kenya

Blue monkey, Lake Manyara, Tanzania

Olive baboon, Maasai Mara, Kenya

Red colobus, Zanzibar

Verreaux's sifaka, Berenty, Madagascar

Vervet monkey, Lake Manyara, Tanzania

Yellow baboon, Amboseli, Kenya

Chimpanzee, Sweetwaters, Kenya

Safari scene, Ndutu, Tanzania ©Arthur Morris 2001

Top 10 Elements in a Great Safari Photograph:

1. Great light. By getting up early and out to the plains, we were able to photograph in the beautiful dawn light.

2. Great subjects. We were surrounded by herds of wildebeest and zebras.

3. Great vehicle. We were in a four-wheel drive Land Rover and therefore able to go off-track among the herds.

4. Careful approach. We wound slowly through the herds and were able to get close without disturbing them.

5. Great equipment. Each photographer had top quality Nikon or Canon equipment to capture this scene.

6. Great execution. The exposure is perfect, the composition is powerful, and the fast shutter speed appears to freeze the stork in mid-air.

7. Great timing. We planned the safari so that we would be in the Serengeti when the herd animals were likely to be giving birth.

8. Perfect light-angle. From our position, the golden light shone right over our shoulders and directly on the animals.

9. Understanding of subject behavior. We parked right next to a white stork flyway.

10. Perfect timing. The stork in flight did not get into the perfect compositional spot by accident.

Long Exposure Blurs

Panning with a bird or animal at slow shutter speeds is a technique that allows motion to be shown in an image. In the following images motion has been illustrated by using a variety of slow shutter speeds. In most cases I set the camera to Shutter Priority and use shutter speeds of from 1/15th to 1/30th of a second. The closer the subject is to the camera, the greater will be the degree of blurring.

Thompson's gazelle and Grant's gazelle, Maasai Mara, Kenya

Impala, Crescent Island, Kenya

Bull Eland, Maasai Mara, Kenya

The stunning sight of a bull Eland perfectly posed in the Maasai Mara grasslands made for a great image. These shy animals, however, require a quiet, cautious approach. The bull was accompanied by a harem of four females each running back and forth to get his attention. When the bull inevitably started chasing them it was simple matter to switch from Aperture Priority to Shutter Priority. I generally set my shutter speed at 1/15th of a second to create blurs similar to the one below. The most pleasing blurs are taken on overcast days where the light is soft and even, and when setting slow shutter speeds is not problematic (as it can be on bright sunny days).

Lesser flamingo flight, Lake Magadi, Ngorongoro Crater, Tanzania

Cheetah and Wildebeest, Ndutu, Tanzania

Photographing Action

One of your primary goals while on safari will be to capture the peak of the action. This is one of the most difficult and challenging skills for a nature photographer to master. Images depicting action are often quite dramatic. The factors that are important to those hoping to capture a defining moment of action include:

1. An intimate knowledge of your equipment.

2. Great anticipation and quick reaction times.

3. Knowledge of a subject's likely behavior; having a good idea (or making an educated guess) as to what is likely to occur.

4. Being in the right place at the right time.

Common zebra, Ngorongoro Crater, Tanzania

Mating lions, Ngorongoro Crater, Tanzania

Playing zebras, Ngorongoro Crater, Tanzania

Secretary bird in flight, Ndutu, Tanzania

Black-backed jackal with Thompson gazelle kill, Maasai Mara, Kenya

Leopard yawn, Ndutu, Tanzania

*Cheetah with impala kill,
Samburu, Kenya*

Lion yawn, Ndutu, Tanzania

Groupings

Early in my safari photography career I took pictures of everything and anything. I would typically carry 300 rolls of film and consider the safari a failure if I didn't use them all. The stylistic decision to focus my efforts on groupings of birds and animals has helped me to become more selective. I try to find groups that are pleasingly arranged in hopes of creating images that work well artistically.

Topi on termite hills, Maasai Mara, Kenya

Cape teal reflections, Ndutu, Tanzania

African great white pelicans, Lake Nakuru, Kenya

Maasai giraffe herd laying in a meadow, Lake Manyara, Tanzania

Juxtapositions

My very first consideration when I approach a subject is the angle of light, followed almost instantly by considering the background. I am a true believer in Arthur Morris' adage: the less distracting the background, the more successful and powerful the image.

Another view of the world presented itself on the 2007 Tanzania Safari. Our van was in the middle of a moving pride of lions. The 2 males flopped onto the grass to groom. In this situation, it is usually only a matter of minutes before they go to sleep and photographic opportunities become extremely limited. The handsome male in the foreground was in

Grey crowned cranes, Ngorongoro Crater

soft light, just perfect for a portrait. The second male was behind him, and, in my mind, was a distraction. Since we were in the middle of the pride we couldn't reposition the van in order to isolate the lion in the front.

A light bulb turned on and I saw the whole scene differently. I realized that if I got lower (by moving my gear to the side window), I could not only include both males in the frame, but the male in the background would be perfectly juxtaposed. Instead of being a distraction, the second lion became a huge asset to the power of the image. For the rest of the safari I searched for similar situations.

Male lions, Ndutu, Tanzania

Southern ground hornbills,
Maasai Mara, Kenya

White storks,
Ndutu, Tanzania

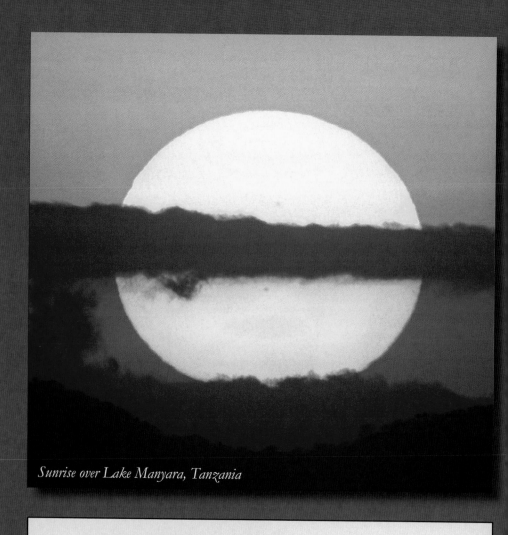
Sunrise over Lake Manyara, Tanzania

Photographing With Long Lenses

All of the photos in this section were taken with *telephoto lenses.*

Most of the photographs that I make on safari are taken with long lenses. My workhorse lens of choice is the 600mm f4 lens. The reach of this lens and the intimacy it provides allows me to fulfill my photographic vision for the vast majority of situations on safari. Using either as a prime lens alone or with teleconverters, the 600 allows me to photograph birds and animals from a safe distance without encroaching on their "flight or fight" zone. My distant second choice is the 200-400mm f4 lens that is usually mounted on my second camera body.

Squacco heron,
Lake Baringo, Kenya

Long lens photography from a safari vehicle, Maasai Mara, Kenya
©Arthur Morris 2006

Nikon On Line Magazine 2004
Long Lens Photography
By Todd Gustafson

"Gee Mister; you sure must have a good camera!" If I had a dime for every time I have gotten this or similar comments, I wouldn't have to sell pictures or write articles ever again. People who see images made with telephoto lenses are universally impressed with the "up close and personal" quality of the photograph. The size and weight of the equipment also raise a lot of eyebrows in the field. For the majority of people, it isn't every day that they see someone in a khaki vest hauling around 75 pounds of gear on a tripod. The truth is that for many nature and wildlife photographers, the telephoto and super telephoto lenses are chosen tools for capturing spectacular, intimate, and emotionally moving images.

The reasons for using super telephotos go beyond their obvious larger magnification. I happen to enjoy bird photography and specialize in East African wildlife. The advantages of using long lenses for what I do are many. One important factor with all wildlife photography (especially bird photography) is the subject's comfort zone. A longer lens allows me a more intimate view from a greater distance. Additionally, even if I can get a closer approach, my very presence affects the bird or animal's behavior and makes for a more static and less natural feeling photograph.

My camera bag includes the Nikon D100* and D1X* bodies, 80-200mm f2.8, 200-400 f4 AF-S zoom and the 600mm f4AF-S lenses. (My "wide angle" lens is the 80-200) I also carry the TC14E, TC17E, TC20E teleconverters and a full set of extension tubes. The extension tubes make the 600mm my favorite macro lens by decreasing the long focus to subject distance inherent in big lenses while making dramatic, frame filling images. At the same time I take advantage of the greater working distance that the super telephoto allows. This isn't crucial when shooting wildflowers, but can be when photographing venomous snakes or shy lizards.

*My how things change.

In the field, there are times when the terrain does not allow a close approach. There may not be a road near the animal or your way may be blocked by rocks or water. It's also difficult to get good shots of birds while climbing the tree to get closer! With the 600mm f4 AF-S I often use teleconverters to achieve even greater magnification and reach. When I can get a close approach, there are times when my rule "You can't get close enough" comes into play. Long lenses with teleconverters give the opportunity to capture priceless expressions as well as textures that resonate with viewers.

A sometimes more important issue of close approach to wild life is the "flight or fight" zone. After leaving a tripod leg section stuck in the mud of Lake Baringo's crocodile infested lake shore, I learned where the crocodile's fight zone was (as well as my flight zone). I was intrigued by the threat display of a 12-foot crocodile, and as I approached on foot, he turned his attention to me. I turned around, planning to move to safer ground, and realized that my tripod leg was stuck in the mud—not attached to the main frame. The croc came barreling out of the lake at me and I ran for it making a mental note to use a 1.4 or a 2x teleconverter the next time I photograph 12-foot crocs! The tripod leg is still there for all I know.

Lesser flamingos, Lake Bogoria, Kenya

Maasai giraffe eyes, Maasai Mara, Kenya

Purple Grenadier, Elsemere, Kenya

Gerenuk, Samburu, Kenya

Common zebras,
Maasai Mara, Kenya

Male kori bustard in display,
Ngorongoro Crater, Tanzania

Cheetah cubs and dik-dik kill, Samburu, Kenya

Lion cubs at play, Ndutu, Tanzania

Lion cub after eating, Ndutu, Tanzania

African open-billed stork, Ndutu, Tanzania

Elephant silhouette, Samburu, Kenya

Red and yellow barbet, Samburu, Kenya

Lion eyes, Maasai Mara, Kenya

Top Ten Tips (plus one) for Safari Success

1. Perform a critical edit of your images every day. Many first time safari photographers plan to bring all their images home to be edited. The number of images captured on a typical safari will usually overload most storage capacity midway through the safari.

2. Zip your tent flap and/or lock the door to your room. Monkeys live around lodge grounds and camps. They are curious and very destructive. They will eat anything, including hard-to-replace medications.

3. Pack efficiently. Bringing too much camera gear can create problems. Transporting all of your heavy, expensive gear to and from East Africa is difficult, as is getting it to and from your room or tent to the van for each safari drive. Some folks have so much gear in the van that it is sometimes difficult to find the required piece of equipment at a moment's notice.

4. Brush your teeth with bottled water. It is not safe to drink tap water in East Africa. Hotels and lodges have bottled water available. The vehicles have bottled water for game drives. Many travelers accidentally make the mistake of drinking or brushing with tap water usually on their first night in Africa when they are tired after their long journey. Be careful out there.

5. Drink lots of water to avoid dehydration. You will often be under a tropical sun for much of the day and the air is dry, so be sure to drink lots of bottled water. It is recommended that you drink at least half your body weight in ounces of water each day to avoid the debilitating effects of dehydration.

6. Wear supportive footwear. Some safaris involve hiking and all demand that you stand for long periods of time while on the game drives. Good quality, light-weight hiking boots are recommended as they offer adequate support. Sneakers, tennis shoes, or sandals are not recommended except for walking to and from meals.

7. Break your shoes in prior to the safari. In many cases, people who have purchased new boots for the safari neglect the importance of breaking in their new footwear. Tired, sore, or blistered feet will result in a less comfortable safari experience.

8. Bend your knees on rough roads and tracks. By bending your knees while traveling over rough park roads or tracks you will lessen the strain on all of your joints.

9. Know your camera equipment. People often purchase new camera equipment just before a safari. Too often, they will bring their new gear on safari without field-testing it or without even reading the manual. It is a good idea to download the PDF of your camera and flash manuals so that you have them on your laptop for quick and easy reference. And be sure to take your new gear into the field for a test drive before you leave for your safari.

10. Keep DEET off your camera equipment. Repellents with DEET will eat away at all types of plastic and can damage the finish of tripods and Wimberley heads. The same goes double for clothing made with synthetic materials.

11. Clean your equipment often. Clean your equipment often. Clean your equipment often. Imagine that there is a gorgeous leopard in your view finder. It is posing perfectly on a great branch and the light is soft and lovely. You depress the shutter button to acquire better focus but your camera will not fire! The leopard jumps from the tree and disappears into the bush…. You chalk it up to being "just one of those things." Later you discover that the front element of your lens has been fogged with a film of safari dust and grit. A twenty-second cleaning with a blower brush or a micro-fiber cloth would have saved the day.

Hunting lions, Lake Manyara, Tanzania

Elephant drinking, Ewaso Ngiro River, Samburu, Kenya

Photographing With Wide Angle Lenses
All of the photographs in this section were taken with wide angle lenses

As you have seen, the great majority of the photographs that I make in
East Africa are made with long telephoto lenses, but there are situations
where a different view presents itself. I like to use an extreme wide angle

lens when there are dramatic skies or a large subject close to the vehicle. Anything from 10.5mm to 24mm (effective 16-35mm) will work well in these situations. Using these wide angle lenses breaks up the continual bombardment of telephoto flavored images when you share your safari photography with friends, clients, or an audience.

Sunrise, Ndutu, Tanzania

106

Squall, Maasai Mara, Kenya

Elephant, Lake Manyara, Tanzania

Acacia tree, storm light, and rainbow, Maasai Mara, Kenya

A Bull elephant, Samburu, Kenya

115

Three Views of the Same Subject

This set of images illustrates a situation where 3 distinctly different photographic views can be equally valid. Flexibility, quick thought, reflexes, and execution all went into this situation. The three photos of this Maasai giraffe were taken within 2 minutes of each other.

The top image was taken with a 17- 35mm 2.8 lens set at 17mm at f22.

The middle photo was taken with an 80-200mm 2.8 lens set at 200mm at f4.

The bottom portrait was taken with a 600mm f4 with a 1.4 teleconverter at f5.6.

Left, middle, right: Maasai giraffe, Maasai Mara, Kenya

Photographing Scenery

All of the photographs in this section were taken with long lenses

The scenic beauty of East Africa is varied and on a vast scale it is perfect for landscape photography. I don't seem to share the vision for wide angle landscapes that others do. Some photographers can create magic with a wide angle lens and a patch of dirt, but I'm not very good at doing that.

Doum palm and volcanic landscape, Samburu, Kenya

I see things differently, preferring to use longer lenses to create my landscape images. Wide angle lenses separate the elements in a photograph and create space and a breathtaking view. I like the way long lenses compress the elements in a scene and allow the viewer an eye level perspective. While on a game drive, I am always looking to the horizon for a dramatic grouping of animals, trees, or light playing across the hills. Again, there is more to photographing in East Africa than large-in-the-frame mammal portraits.

Doum palm in at sunrise, Samburu, Kenya

Yellow-bark acacia and euphorbia candelabra forest, Lake Nakuru, Kenya

Balloon at sunrise, Maasai Mara, Kenya

Practical Considerations
Mosquitoes
Mosquitoes in Africa carry diseases and parasites including malaria and yellow fever. Depending on conditions in East Africa, Yellow fever can be an issue, as can malaria. There are effective anti-malaria prophylactics that you that you really must take. Consult your physician when making pre-safari medical decisions.

Mosquito populations flourish in wet ecosystems and are diminished in dry conditions or at higher elevations. Apply repellent and wear long sleeve shirts and pants in the early evening. Dark clothing, according to some, may attract biting insects, so a light toned khaki wardrobe works well while on safari.

Lodge rooms in mosquito areas will usually have mosquito nets over the beds to protect you while you sleep. Use them. Bugs are attracted to light, so turn your room light off before you go to dinner. I have, on occasion, forgotten to do this and have returned to the room only to be greeted by a number of flying visitors. When this occurs, I spray my room (I am sure to spray under the bed), turn off the lights, and take a walk back to the lounge while the spray dissipates. When I return to the room, there are no more bugs and I can sleep in peace.

Tsetse Flies
Not all tsetse flies carry sleeping sickness. Of those that do, some affect humans, while others affect livestock. The type that inhabit parts of the national parks affect livestock and are, in reality, a good thing for the wildlife. Domesticated cattle and goats cannot be grazed in the huge areas of the country where these flies live, thereby diminishing pressure on the parks.

If you get bitten by one of these flies you will most definitely feel it! You will be aware of them and try to brush them away as you would a fly at home. The problem is that they hang on and aren't intimidated by your feeble attempts to shoo them away. The trick is to wear long sleeve shirts and pants in tsetse fly areas.

Medical Issues
Insulin and refrigerated medications can be stored in the lodge kitchen refrigerator.

Travelers with sleep apnia have, in the past, brought a rechargeable battery system to operate their CPap equipment.

Taking Precautions Against the Sun and the Heat

Most safari itineraries include lots of time spent at higher altitudes, usually between 3,000 and 7,500 feet, and the equatorial sun can be quite strong. The air is often crisp and clear, and there is often a cool breeze. People are surprised when they come in from a day of photographing and have fierce sunburns. Remember to bring a wide-brimmed hat or a safari hat with drapes and sunscreen of SPF 30 or more and use them. Wearing long sleeve shirts and long pants will also protect your skin, especially if they are made of sun protective material of SPF 30 or more. You are far better protecting yourself from the sun with suitable clothing than with chemicals.

In some locations like Tarangire National Park in Tanzania, however, it can be quite hot, so you must take steps to prevent heat exhaustion. Dry air can dehydrate the body dramatically, and dehydration can lead to heat exhaustion or heatstroke. It is imperative that you drink lots of bottled water, and wear loose-fitting clothing (so your body can best dissipate heat). If it is sunny and hot and you begin to feel weak, dizzy, or nauseous, get out of the sun, drink lots of water, and put a cool compress on your forehead. Getting out of the sun on a safari drive may entail clearing a seat and sitting down out of the sun or even getting into the front passenger seat next to your driver.

This safari photographer illustrates good roof hatch photo technique and is wearing long sleeves and a hat for sun protection.

On Location

Exploring the Grounds of Camps and Lodges

All of the photographs in this section were made on the grounds of lodges or camps in Tanzania and Kenya.

I structure my safari itinerary very carefully to include lodges and camps with plenty of photographic subjects on the grounds. To me, it is disappointing to finish a morning game drive and return to a lodge where there are no birds or animals to see and photograph during the midday and afternoon hours.

When the game drive is over and you have downloaded all of your images, it doesn't mean that the morning's photography is done. Quality images can often be made at your camp or lodge if you take advantage of the opportunities (and if you have the energy to do so). You can sometimes find fantastic subjects by walking the grounds, setting up your tripod and a big lens as you read a book on the porch, or even by setting up a feeder while having a drink at the bar.

I have spent hours walking the grounds of camps and lodges searching for photographic subjects. All of these accommodations are either inside or adjacent to national parks and reserves. The species available at a given site is an important factor in my choice of lodges. Birds, flowers, reptiles, bats, and monkeys often live on or pass through these grounds.

Before walking the grounds on you own, first check with the front desk to see if there is a resident naturalist who can provide either guided nature walks or information. These walks often operate during game drive times so you should ask if you can arrange to do a private walk with a guide. You may need to pay a fee. If this is not the case, you should tip the guide for sharing his time and expertise. If the lodge does not have a naturalist on staff, you can still talk to the lodge personnel about what and where some good subjects might be located. The lodge staff always works hard to make your stay as comfortable, enjoyable, and as productive as possible. They stay out of a guest's way and go about their business quietly. Try the Swahili greeting "Jambo, habari yako?" (Hello, how are you?) With this greeting you have introduced yourself as a person worth talking to. Allow a new acquaintance to look through your long lens and take a picture. You may have just made a friend who might be happy to share his/her knowledge with you.

Friendly staff members have taken me to doves on eggs, sleeping bats, perched owls (African Scops Owl, Pearl spotted Owlet, Verroux's Eagle Owl) and nesting Hooded Vultures. Being especially friendly to the staff persons may pay unexpected dividends. I got to photograph a mongoose burrow on the grounds of Amboseli's Ol Tukai Lodge because my room steward was kind enough to share his knowledge with me. (Mongooses are welcome residents at the lodges because they eat snakes and insects).

Grey-headed kingfisher, Lake Manyara, Tanzania

Golden palm weaver, Malindi, Kenya

Safari Tale # 10

After photographing some Golden Palm Weavers in the lodge gardens, I was approached by an Italian gentleman who had been sitting by the pool. He had seen me working by the nests and told me he was going on safari with his family after their beach holiday. "Could you give me some help with my camera?" I agreed, and was amazed when he brought a beautiful 35mm camera and spectacular lens for me to look at. They were still in the box! His first question to me as he held up the 400mm lens was, "What is this?"

I did my best, with the limited time available, to help him prepare for his foray into the game parks, but I had some misgivings about his chances for success. It was gratifying to be able to help Mr. Martini learn some of the fundamentals of photography; an hour well-spent by the pool of the beach resort.

I could only hope that he didn't have too many high expectations for the pictures he hoped to capture.

Lesson: *Get comfortable with your equipment before you leave on safari and always be nice to people.*

African grey hornbill feeding, Elsamere, Kenya

Yellow-billed stork, Lake Naivasha, Kenya

Three-banded plover, Lake Naivasha, Kenya

135

Grey heron, Lake Naivasha, Kenya

Spectacled weaver,
Lake Naivasha, Kenya

Pied kingfisher, Lake Naivasha, Kenya

Sacred ibis, Lake Naivasha, Kenya

Male Mwanza flat-headed agama, Maasai Mara, Kenya

African scops owl, Maasai Mara, Kenya

Nile monitor lizard, Samburu, Kenya

Egyptian goose and goslings, Lake Baringo, Kenya

Marabou stork sunning, Lake Baringo, Kenya

Pearl-spotted owlet, Samburu, Kenya

African paradise flycatcher, Lake Baringo, Kenya

Vervet monkey, Samburu, Kenya

146

IMPORTANT

SAFETY WARNING

Before heading out on your own to photograph on the grounds of your lodge or tented camp for the first time, check with the front desk regarding any safety information that may be relevant to your location. There could be places on the grounds where it would not be safe to walk alone. There may be a wildlife trail going through or adjacent to the camp. There may be a river on the property where unseen crocodiles or hippos may lurk. Pay attention to signs that say things like "Wildlife can be dangerous," or "Guests not allowed beyond this point." These signs are not just for show. If you have a guide with you, he will watch for any possible dangers and point out subjects of interest to you.

Lake Baringo in flood

Safari Tale #11

Art and I were photographing on the shores of Lake Baringo in 1997, the year of El Nino and great flooding. Water levels were very high and much of the grounds were under water. Nile cabbage-covered water was 150 yards past the lake shore of previous years, creating a beautiful, subject-filled environment.

The usually shy squacco herons, African jacanas, and kingfishers were all within photographic range. We wanted to get a bit closer to a grey-headed kingfisher on a nice perch out in the Nile cabbage; Art asked if we could wade through the shallow water to get closer. .

My answer was, "I'm pretty sure there are crocs in the lake."

"I don't see any," was Art's reply.

"Maybe we should ask…"

At that moment, not 20 feet away, a 12 foot Nile crocodile burst out of the Nile Cabbage with an 18" tilapia in his mouth. It was—to say the least—heart stopping!

Lesson: *Check with the hotel staff with regards to safety issues in and around the camp. Assume that danger may lurk in the areas that you explore, and err on the side of caution.*

Blue-headed tree Agama, Ndutu, Tanzania

Male baboon threat display, Tarangire Tented Camp, Tanzania

Opting to Rest

As a safari progresses, it is possible that you may become extremely fatigued, too weak and tired to be productive on a game drive. If you feel that this might be happening to you, consider skipping a game drive. Be sure to let one of the leaders know that you will be staying at the lodge. This is especially important if you will be missing a morning game drive as time and early morning light are of the essence. After a nap you will be refreshed and feel more like exploring the grounds with your camera.

These baboon photos were taken when I opted to skip an afternoon game drive. We were staying at the Tarangire Tented Camp, which is set on a ridge overlooking the Tarangire River valley. The grounds there can provide great photographic opportunities at all times of day. While walking back to my tent and admiring the view, a group of tourists staying at the lodge directed my attention to the "big baboon" sitting on a low wall. While I have more than my share of baboon images, I pointed my camera at the baboon just to be polite. Just as the subject came into focus he bared his teeth in a threat display directed at a nearby adult baboon. It seemed as if my subject wanted the other animal to stay clear of the female and baby in the accompanying photo.

I was quick to share the images I had made with the folks who pointed out the baboon on the camera's LCD; they were as thrilled as I was.

My photography that day was in no way compromised by missing the game drive. In addition, I was well rested and had time to clean my equipment and to charge my batteries.

Speckled mousebirds, Maasai Mara, Kenya

Northern masked weaver, Lake Baringo, Kenya

Vervet monkey kiss, Samburu, Kenya

Speckle-fronted weaver, Lake Manyara, Tanzania

The Safari Nap

All of the photographs in this section were taken during "Safari Naps."

One of my top secret-weapons for in-camp photography is what I call the "Safari Nap." I use capital letters to emphasize the importance of this event. If you are tired, it is almost always best to take a nap. Photographing on safari can be exhausting work. Pre-dawn departures on game drives, new experiences, stimulating subject matter, standing throughout game drives, and rough and dusty roads can all take their toll on you. You need to take care of yourself. Taking the time for a "safari nap" can benefit you both physically and mentally.

Before you take a nap, look at the area just outside your tent or room. Are there any trees, logs, or rocks that might make a suitable perch for a photograph if a bird were to land on it? Are there lizards that come to a specific rock to sun themselves? Set up your tripod (with a camera and a big lens on it) outside of your tent flap or on the porch of your room. It should be placed so that you have a good view of the most likely perches without moving the equipment.

Now you can take a nap. The quiet of a lodge during the off hours is such that the flutter of a bird's wings, or the rustle of leaves as a lizard passes by, are clearly audible. If you hear something promising while you are resting, it is easy to go outside and make a picture or two. With the equipment already in place you are unlikely to disturb your subject.

Yellow-spotted bush hyrax, Serana Lodge, Maasai Mara, Kenya

160

African paradise flycatcher, Sarova Camp, Maasai Mara

Southern black flycatcher, Saburu Lodge, Samburu, Kenya

Ashy starling, Tarangire Tented Camp, Tanzania

Rainbow skink, Island Camp, Lake Baringo, Kenya

Nile monitor lizard, Island Camp, Lake Baringo, Kenya

Safari Tale #12

Our safari group was staying at Island Camp in the middle of Kenya's Lake Baringo. The entire area represents the quintessential Rift Valley lake environment. Photography here is done either from a boat out on the lake, or on the grounds of the camp. My tent, which faced the lake, was on a small rock outcrop under an acacia tree. I had noticed that a skink (a small, striped lizard) lived under my porch and liked to sun on a nearby rock. My goal was to have my camera set up during my nap so that I could quietly get into shooting position without disturbing the lizard.

During my nap I heard the leaves rustling, and I thought "Here he comes." I thought the sounds were a little loud for a 9" Skink but wasn't too concerned. I decided to give him about 5 minutes to get comfortable. Instead of quieting down to sun on the rock, the noise got louder and closer. I hadn't zipped the flap of my tent so that I could get in and out quietly. As I waited for the skink to settle, the unzipped flap opened and the head of a 5 foot Nile monitor lizard appeared! As I tell my son, I jumped up on the bed and screamed. The startled monitor lizard made a quick exit. I followed him out and headed for my tripod. As he stopped for a moment at the top of a small rise, I was able to make one beautiful portrait before he disappeared into the bush.

Lesson: *Have your equipment at hand and ready to use and keep your ears open while sleeping.*

Setting up a Perch and Feeder

All photos in this section were made at feeders.

Many species of bush birds live in or around the camps and lodges. They are accustomed to people walking the grounds and aren't bothered too much by photographers. Most of the lodges have a rock or concrete feeder where they put day-old bread and fruit; the birds are always ready to take advantage of a free meal. When the kitchen staff puts out a free meal, the birds literally rain out of the sky a-la Alfred Hitchcock!

At first, this might seem like a great situation for photography, but in reality, the opposite is true. Most of the feeders are placed in locations with filtered or bright light, or in spots with horribly cluttered backgrounds. With so many birds in the area, it is difficult, if not impossible to find a single bird on a clean, natural perch. The cement feeders are ugly and even the natural stone feeders have crusts of bread and a fruit cup left-over-from-lunch. To add insult to injury, the multitude of birds can clean out a huge bounty of food in a matter of minutes, leaving the photographer with a dazed look on his or her face and not a single photograph.

The ideal situation would be to have single birds landing on clean perches with distant, uniform backgrounds while the photographer sits in the shade with a cold Coca-Cola (or better yet, a cold Fanta Passion) in hand. Crazy at it may sound; this can often be done in a matter of minutes with great success. Talk to the management staff and see if they would mind if you set up some temporary perches. Then collect some interesting looking branches that would be suitable perches for the species likely to visit your feeder.

The feeder should be in an open, shady area with no distracting shafts of sunlight glaring through. Ideally, it will offer one or two spots where the background is a good distance from the feeder. Erect or tape the perches in place and you will find that the birds will land on them when they first drop down to check out their free meal. (The perches can be wedged into rocks, put into the ground, or secured with the duct tape you brought in your checked luggage—see Packing List).

Now you are ready to put the food out and wait for the birds to arrive. If you put out all the food at once, the birds will show up and quickly take all the food, leaving you precious little time to shoot. The solution is to dole out the food sparingly. Each time you put out a bit more food the birds will fly into the surrounding bushes and wait for you to get back behind your camera. Then they will fly back to the perches before descending on the food again. You will come to recognize individual birds and be ready for them to land on a favored perch. Keep your eyes on the surrounding bushes, as well. There will often be a host of shy birds waiting for their chance at the free meal. You can often get permission from the lodge management to trim a few branches to create another perfect perch or two. And if

Blue-naped mousebird, Island Camp, Lake Baringo, Kenya

the conditions at the established feeder make it impossible to create any decent images, you can often get permission to set up an impromptu feeder at a more suitable location. In any case, you can spend many relaxing hours at a feeder set-up making stunning images of otherwise hard-to-photograph birds.

One of my favorite perches was set up by Arthur Morris at Lake Baringo Island Camp. We were actually photographing beautiful birds on great perches in perfect light with clear, distant backgrounds while sitting in the shade of the bar with a cold Coke in hand!

I am not an expert at feeders but have had success at setting them up using Art's suggestions. For more on setting up feeders, get Arthur Morris' *"The Art of Bird Photography"* and *"The Art of Bird Photography 2"* available through birdsasart.com or e-mail at birdsasart@verizon.net

Cut-throat finch, Sopa Lodge, Samburu, Kenya

Red fronted barbet,
Island Camp, Lake Baringo, Kenya

169

Jackson's golden-backed weaver, Island Camp, Lake Baringo, Kenya

Dark-capped bulbul, Island Camp, Lake Baringo, Kenya

Photographing From a Boat

All of the images in this section were created on boat rides on Rift Valley lakes.

There is a string of lakes in the Great Rift Valley that support multiple ecosystems. The number of birds and the variety of species found at these lakes makes them great for photography. Each lake has different terrain and water chemistry, and each of them supports between 350 and 500 bird species.

The best way to photograph many of these birds is from a boat in the morning. Almost without exception, the wind is calmest and the water smoothest in the early morning. By the afternoon, rising winds and the resulting waves usually make photography impossible.

Most of the lodges have several 24 foot, 6-person fiberglass boats for outings on the lake. They can be propelled with the outboard motor or with a push pole for silent maneuvering. In boats of this type, it is best to have no more than three photographers per boat. They are not perfectly stable and rock easily when people shift their weight. They are, however, light and draw little water so they can easily negotiate the shallows. With a skilled boat-driver, it is often easy to get very close to the birds; this can result in some excellent close-quarters photography. It is absolutely magical to drift toward the shore and have the boat bottom out on a sand bank 15 feet from a Malachite Kingfisher.

To set up in the types of boat shown here, I extend two of the tripod's legs half way, spread them out to the widest position, and place them on the gunnels with the ends of the legs out over the sides. Then I point the third leg straight down to the floor of the boat and adjust the length of this leg so that the camera's eye piece is just a bit below my eye level. This way I can pan left or right and comfortably point the lens a bit downwards where many of the subjects will be.

Your guides, the boatmen, work for the hotels. Like your safari drivers, they know where the birds and animals are most likely to be found. Make a list of what you hope to photograph and compare it to what the boatman thinks you are most likely to see, and then decide on a plan. It can be difficult for a boatman to hear directions or instructions about how to approach subjects so before you leave the dock work out a series of simple arm signals for: left, right, circle, slow the boat, and stop the boat. And be sure to let him know that if the engine is running when you give the signal to stop that you would like him to shut the engine off immediately. If your boatman does a good job, a nice tip is—of course—in order at the end of the photo-cruise.

Covered fiberglass boat, Lake Baringo, Kenya

Open fiberglass boat, Lake Baringo, Kenya

I cannot overstate the importance of being as still as possible in the boat and keeping your movements to an absolute minimum so I have repeated this advice here. While the advice may seem obvious, you may not realize how important it is until you are actually in the boat with a long telephoto lens on your tripod. As the movement of the boat will be multiplied by the square of the effective focal length of your lens, all movements and even small vibrations will result in unsharp images. In addition, it is likely that if the boat is rocking at all, it will be difficult to find the subject in the viewfinder and at times, impossible to keep it in the frame. Even the act of changing a flash card or switching tele-converters can—and will—cause the boat to rock unless you are both aware and careful. Multiply by three or four and you can get an idea of just how much extra rocking can be generated.

Large open fiberglass boat, Lake Baringo, Kenya

Super telephoto rig set up for boat photography

Covered fiberglass boat, Lake Baringo, Kenya

MK 413 N
CABIN CRUISER
LAKE NAIVASHA COUNTRY CLUB

Covered pontoon boat, Lake Naivasha, Kenya

Only one person, the boat leader, should give the arm signals to avoid confusion. You can then go out on the lake and see what's out there.

When you are photographing from a boat, try—as you would in a safari van—to move in super-slow motion when you need to make equipment changes and try to make them as the boat is approaching the subject so that you can be completely still when it is time to begin making images. If everyone in the boat concentrates on being as still as possible and maintaining his or her balance while seated, the entire experience will be enhanced and the photographic returns can be spectacular.

Eye level shot of a hippo taken from a boat, Lake Naivasha, Kenya

Subjects that you are most likely to encounter include as many as eight species of kingfisher, eighteen species of herons and egrets (including the world's largest heron, the aptly named Goliath heron), African fish eagles, many species of weavers nesting, and African jacana, to name just a few. You may also get to photograph hippo and crocodile at eye level. They are typically shy and obviously dangerous so be sure to photograph them from a safe distance.

Safari Tale #13

I make sure that every Kenya safari itinerary that I create includes a stay at one or more lake camps or lodges. The photo opportunities with Rift Valley lake ecosystem birds are unparalleled and the experience of photographing them is completely different from typical game drive photography. Long-time friend and safari photographer, Tom Tyler, would rather photograph from a boat than do any other type of safari photography. He points out that the percentage of quality photos made per hour from a boat on an East African lake far exceeds what you can do while walking the grounds or photographing from a vehicle and he cites his experiences at Lake Baringo to prove his point. This shallow lake has lots of crocs and lots of tilapia for them to eat. The tilapia dig holes in the bed of the lake to protect their nests and eggs from the crocs (and from birds that hunt along the lake shore).

After a particularly productive morning boat ride at Lake Baringo, Tom was eager to get more time on the lake. After lunch he asked if anyone wanted to join him on an afternoon boat ride. Another photographer immediately volunteered. I reminded them that if the wind came up that the resulting chop would make photography impossible. "How bad could it be?" were the last words I heard as they headed for the dock.

I wandered the grounds for a while and made my way back to my room for a nap. On the way, I met a water-logged Tom coming back from the dock.

"What happened?"

He said that the wind had come up and that with the waves were so choppy it was impossible to photograph. (Does that sound familiar?)

They decided to come back to shore after just five minutes, but the wind turned the boat parallel to the shore. The wave pattern trapped the boat thirty feet from shore for more than half an hour. Crocodiles were scattered in the water about them, heading toward the shore for afternoon sunning. Eventually, the second passenger said "Enough is enough," and hopped over the side of the boat. The shallow water reached only to his knees and he walked to shore ignoring the crocodiles.

Tom decided to follow his lead and hopped out on the other side of the boat. Instead of landing in two feet of water Tom stepped directly into a tilapia nest and sank up to his armpits holding $14,000.00 worth of camera equipment above his head! The boatman grabbed his equipment and hauled him out of the hole. After that, Tom was able to make his way safely back to shore.

Lesson: *Take boat rides only in the morning.*

Yellow-billed storks at sunrise, Lake Baringo, Kenya

Crocodile eye taken from a boat, Lake Baringo, Kenya

Hippo yawn, Lake Naivasha, Kenya

African spoonbill, Lake Naivasha, Kenya

Calling African fish eagle, Lake Naivasha, Kenya

Pied kingfisher, Lake Baringo, Kenya

Gibralta Island, Lake Baringo Kenya

Malachite kingfisher,

Goliath heron

African white pelican

Photographing African Fish Eagles

Photographing an African Fish Eagle catching a fish is a great challenge. Tilapia fishermen on the lake will bring fish to the boat and sell them for a few shillings. Your boatman will first get an eagle's attention with a high-pitched whistle and then throw the fish. The eagles glide in and grab the fish out of the water.

They usually live as pairs so at each stop you will generally have two chances. If you miss the shot on the two passes you will have to find another pair because the eagles will be dining on your fish for the next hour. It is always best to be prepared.

Preparations Should Include:

1. Checking out the wind direction relative to the sun-angle: If the sun and the wind are from the same direction, the bird will be flying towards you and towards the light; such conditions are ideal. If the wind is blowing towards the sun you will need to try and make your pictures as the bird flies towards you; if you wait until the bird banks back into the wind to grab the fish, you will wind up with butt-shots.

2. Thinking through the exposure: The bird has dark, chestnut-colored wings and a pure white head like a Bald Eagle. In addition, as the bird approaches the boat, the background will be changing rapidly. Each background will affect the metering system differently so it is unlikely that you will get a good exposure for each image.

The solution to this problem is to use Manual mode. You need to determine a correct exposure so as not to overexpose the bird's white bird's head. In morning sunlight you can add 1/3 or 2/3 of a stop of light to the meter reading that you get off the blue sky 30 degrees up from the horizon (depending on your camera). Once you have done this, you can photograph the birds against different backgrounds without having to worry about the exposure.

3. Deciding what lens to use: If you want a photo of one of these majestic birds steaming right towards the boat you will need to use your long lens. If you want to try and capture the moment of the strike or the eagle emerging with the fish you will need an intermediate telephoto zoom lens. The group will need to discuss exactly where and how far they would like the boat driver to throw the fish. You can then use the lens that will best help you create the image that you want. Being prepared is the key as it will all be over in a matter of seconds once the bird gets anywhere near the boat.

The top photograph was taken with a 300mm lens. The fish was thrown 40 feet from the boat. The bottom photo was taken with a 600mm lens. The fish was 100 feet away, thrown from a second boat.

Njemps fisherman in balsa boat, Lake Baringo, Kenya.

The trees along the shores of Lake Baringo provide a balsa-like wood from which the Njemps tribesmen make their boats. They fish the lake for tilapia. These fish can be purchased for a few shillings and used to feed the African fish eagles. A small piece of the extremely lightweight wood is sewn in place

in the fish's gut to prevent it from sinking. The boatmen make a whistling call to get the eagles' attention before throwing the fish. It all sounds rather simple but in reality the shifting winds often make the bird's approach unpredictable, and at times, a second eagle will come in from an unexpected angle and steal the fish.

African Fish Eagles, Lake Baringo, Kenya

Photographing From a Balloon

All images in this section were taken from a balloon.

At a cost of about USD450.00 per person, a balloon ride in East Africa is an expensive proposition, but the experience can be spectacular. The best time of day for a game drive is also the very best for a balloon ride. People are often hesitant about booking such an expensive option. When they finally decide to go, all of the spots are often filled. If taking a balloon ride is something that you would really like to do, try to arrange for your flight early in your safari so that you are guaranteed a spot in the gondola.

Balloons take off early; the guides from the balloon company will arrive to transport you to the balloon at about 5:30 AM. With 12-16 passengers in the gondola hand-held lenses are the only option. I would suggest anything from a fish eye lens to a mid-range telephoto zoom lens. Wide angle lenses are great for making photos featuring both the vast savannah and the sky. I use my Nikon 80-400 VR lens to photograph groups of animals below the balloon. The shorter mid-range zooms are useful for creating scenic images with huge herds of animals in them. From the air, shadows become an important part of the scene, so be aware of them as you are planning your compositions.

As the balloon travels through the air, it is rotating slowly to ensure that nobody is in the best spot. Different compositions will unfold before your eyes very quickly; you must stay on your toes in order to create some pleasing images. Your perspective changes constantly and the balloon cannot stop like a safari vehicle can. You must quickly learn to scan from under the balloon to the horizon and to design your images on the fly.

The balloons need to put down within a relatively small area that depends in part upon park boundaries and even national borders; the entire journey is based on the direction and the speed of the wind. The greater the wind speed, the shorter your balloon ride will be. As the balloon lands, the gondola slides across the ground quite rapidly and the basket usually tips over. It is important that you have your camera and lenses safely stowed in vest pockets or in a small camera bag so that they aren't damaged during landing.

A ground vehicle will have been following the flight and will radio the rest of the team to join you at the landing site. This vehicle will then take you on a short game drive while the rest of the team sets up a champagne breakfast. The game drive, while short, may be interesting because it is likely that the landing area is an area that you have not visited on game drives. After the game drive, you will get to enjoy a full-scale breakfast in the middle of an East African game park. A champagne breakfast is certainly not mandatory on a photo safari but it surely is a nice touch!

Early morning balloon inflation, Mara Serena, Maasai Mara

Balloon and Topi, Maasai Mara, Kenya

Balloon shadow over wildebeest, Maasai Mara, Kenya

Views of the great migration from a balloon, Maasai Mara, Kenya

View of the great migration from a balloon, Maasai Mara, Kenya

More views of the great migration from a balloon, Maasai Mara, Kenya

Wildebeest herd from a balloon, Maasai Mara, Kenya

Photographers in a balloon gondola, Maasai Mara, Kenya

Champagne and brunch toast on landing, Maasai Mara, Kenya

Time Management

A Typical Safari Day

When people go on their first safari, as with any first, they do not have an accurate picture in their minds of how it will all work. Some people have the ability to let the chips fall as they may, while others worry about the unknown. Almost all will say later in the trip "I wish I had known that" about some aspect of the safari. People often think when you are on safari you get in a van and drive around all day taking pictures of animals. In this section, you will find several possibilities as to what a typical safari day might be like.

The Night Before

I start the discussion here because the night before is when one must prepare his equipment for the next day. Make sure your lenses, your camera bodies, and the sensors of your digital cameras are clean, and make sure that all of your batteries are charged. All my rechargeable electronics are plugged into a Todd-Plug each evening. These include camera batteries, AA batteries, a Quantum 2X2, and my lap top computer among others. By doing this religiously every night, I know that I will start the next day with everything fully charged and that I can sleep in peace. (Make it a habit to grab your stuff off the chargers each morning!).

If there is a game drive scheduled for the next morning, I will have my camera and lens setup on the Todd-Pod ready to go. (Some photographers prefer to mount their lens on the Todd-Pod when they get in the safari van). If the day is to start off with a walk on the grounds, I will have my gear set up on a tripod and my vest packed with the appropriate equipment. If the day begins with a boat ride, my rig, already on the tripod, will be ready to go as soon as I grab my vest.

Early Wake-up

All of the photos in this section were taken before dawn.

Since I know that my equipment is prepared in advance, I wake up a little before 6:00 and get dressed for the day (while others usually are up a bit earlier). A typical morning in up-country game parks of East Africa can be fairly chilly, so I wear long pants and a couple of layers of shirts. As it warms up, the extra shirts can be taken off. I put all of the recharged batteries in the equipment, attach my Quantum 2X2, and head to the dining hall for a cup of tea prior to entering the safari vehicle. In most game parks, you are not allowed on the roads until 6:30 am; the goal is to be loaded and out of the gate by 6:30. (See the "Safari Time Is Precious" section).

While driving around taking pictures of animals is pretty much why we are on safari, there is a lot more to it than that. Peak times for animal activity and light quality are critical considerations when working out a schedule. On clear days the hours from predawn until 8:30 am or so are usually when you will find the best light and active birds and animals, waking up to start the day.

214

Lion cub, Ngorongoro Crater, Tanzania

The animals' morning activities tell their life stories; they are waking, stretching, eating, drinking, or playing as they start the new day. Photographs of these activities often depict the most powerful and inspirational moments of the safari. The first light of a new day has the color and drama most desired by photographers.

The vast majority of people who go on safari are not photographers. Their schedule usually goes something like this: 7:00 am wake up, 8:00 breakfast with an 8:30 or 9:00 safari drive start. On many days, the serious photographers will have the entire park to themselves during prime time. Oftentimes, as we are driving back to the lodge, we will see other groups just beginning their game drives.

By 8:30 or 9:00 am, the heat of the day begins to build and the animals tend to head to for cover to get out of the sun and rest. Most animals and birds become far less active, and the light gets harsher by the minute. Hard shadows make for poor photographs. On cloudy or overcast days, the photography can be productive for the rest of the day. The animals do not need to find shade, and the light remains soft and diffused; contrast is low and there are no distracting shadows.

Young lion cubs and mother, Ngorongoro Crater, Tanzania

Cape Buffalo and spotted hyena, Ngorongoro Crater, Tanzania

Yellow-bark acacia trees in morning mist, Lake Nakuru, Kenya

Lesser Flamingos, Lake Nakuru, Kenya

Sunrise over Ngorongoro Crater, Tanzania

Common zebras at dawn, Ngorongoro Crater, Tanzania

Wildebeest drinking, Ngorongoro Crater, Tanzania

Breakfast

All photos in this section were taken during breakfast

The kitchen staff stops serving breakfast between 9:00 and 9:30 so the drivers normally need to return to the lodge a bit before that. If it is overcast, folks may opt to skip breakfast and stay out in the park to photograph, but you cannot do that unless everyone in the vehicle agrees. While that seems like a good solution, you must consider your drivers. They have gotten up early and driven for several hours. It isn't fair to them to have to skip breakfast in hopes of your finding something else to photograph. It also isn't fair to the lodge staff to have to wait for you past 9:30.

My favorite meal on safari is breakfast. Coming back from a successful game drive to fresh fruit juice, pancakes, made-to-order omelets and a cup of tea is tough to beat! When the pattern has been cloudy, overcast weather, the best strategy, however, is to have your drivers arrange for boxed breakfasts the night before the game drive. By doing this you can remain in the park and make images at your leisure. There is no pre set time to be back in camp.

Folks can either grab a box breakfast and eat on the fly, or the group can decide to stop the van and enjoy breakfast. Try to find a place where there may be photographic possibilities, like a hippo pool or a watering hole. Another option would be to stop in the midst of a zebra or wildebeest herd. You may enjoy a spectacular show while you dine. I put my box breakfast on the roof right next to my rig so that all I have to do is put down the pastry and shoot.

Different lodges pack their breakfasts in different ways. Some tie all of the boxes together in a large plastic bag. Others put all of the breakfast components into large picnic baskets. Both of these styles require that all the vans in your safari group meet at a specific location in order to eat. This can lead to a pleasant experience in a beautiful spot where people from different vans share stories of the day. The huge drawback with both of these systems is that some vans may be in the middle of photographing a great subject or situation and get the call that it's time to head to the breakfast spot. At that point they have to leave their subject and drive across the park to the site. This can be very frustrating.

Talk to your drivers after every afternoon game drive and devise a plan for the next day. Make sure that there are enough breakfast boxes (along with thermoses of coffee and tea and all the fixings) in each van. Then the drivers can arrange for the correct number of breakfast boxes to be distributed to each van. Doing this the night before allows the kitchen time to plan for the next day's breakfasts.

Hippos sparring, Mara River, Maasai Mara

Hippos sparring, Mara River, Maasai Mara

Breakfast, Serengeti National Park, Tanzania

Egyptian goose, Ngorongoro Crater, Tanzania

African land snail, Tarangire, Tanzania

Millipede, Tarangire, Tanzania

Running wildebeest, 1000th of a second shutter speed, Ndutu, Tanzania

Wildebeest and zebra migration, Ndutu, Tanzania

Running wildebeest, 20th of a second shutter speed, Ndutu, Tanzania

Back at the Lodge

The game drive is over and you are back at the lodge or camp. What now? When we used film the answer was easy....refill your pockets with film, take a nap, or go for a swim. Life was easy and relaxing. The drawback was that we didn't know with real certainty what we had photographed on that game drive. With digital technology, post game drive time is filled with a long to-do list.

As we approach the lodge, I pack my photo gear in my camera bag and make sure that the seats are clear of my things. This way I can exit the vehicle quickly and safely without the people who are sitting behind me having to wait for me.

The first thing I do when I get back to my room is put all of my batteries in the chargers and start downloading the compact flash cards. When I am finished with a game drive, I know exactly which cards I have used. Clean cards are stored in the case face up. When I have filled a card with images, I put the full card back in the case face down. I remove the full cards from the case and keep track of them by placing them face down on the left side of my computer (the side that my card reader is on). After each card is downloaded, I put them face up back in the case. Develop a routine for downloading the images on your cards to ensure that you do not re-format a card that has not been downloaded. (The very best way to do this it to look at the images on a given card before formatting the card; do not format it if you have not seen the images on your laptop. If you are in doubt, grab another card and check things out when you get back. Better safe than sorry).

As discussed previously, the next order of business is to thoroughly clean my cameras and lenses using a camel hair brush, a micro fiber cloth, and the Lens Pens. (I use the large Lens Pen to clean the visible and accessible surfaces of my lenses and teleconverters while the small Lens Pen is reserved for sensor cleaning). You can chip away at these tasks as your cards download.

Everyone has his own order of doing business, and if a system works for you, do it that way every time to avoid mixing up your CF cards. Now that the morning's shoot is over, your equipment has been taken care of, and your files have been downloaded, you can take some time to relax. I like to have a soda and a snack while I take a look at the results of the morning's shoot.

Critical Daily Editing

Other than capturing the images, the most important travel photography issue for me is the editing process. One reason for this is the limited disc space available while traveling on safari. Clearing disc space can become a major issue for photographers who do not edit critically each and every day. With image files getting bigger with each new camera model, storage space is continually at a premium.

Many first time safari photographers come to me in a panic telling me that they are out of disc space. This usually happens around the middle of the safari. I ask if they have been doing their daily edits. The answer is almost universally "No. I wanted to wait till I got home to do that." They are most concerned about saving "record shots" of species they have never seen or photographed before. When asked how many record shots they are keeping the answer is usually 20-30 per new species... I advise them to keep one or two record shots of each new species and to try to improve on those images as the safari progresses.

To me, editing ruthlessly is more than an exercise in clearing disc space. Seeing the images that you have created on the same day that you made them can be a great springboard for artistic development. You can decide what you liked about a given image and try to create similar images of other animals and birds. You can also note the elements in a photograph that bother you and strive to eliminate them in future photographs. You will know when you have created the image that you have envisioned. This will allow you to move on to new and different subjects without wasting time chasing a subject that you have already photographed well. (If, however, you find the same subject in a great situation be sure to take advantage of it).

Another benefit of daily ruthless editing is that you will know what subjects you have not photographed well. Most of the game parks and national reserves have specialty species that are relatively common there or endemic to that area. Kenya's Samburu National Reserve is a perfect example of this; it is famous for gerenuk, reticulated giraffe, beisa oryx, Grevy's zebra, vulturine Guinea-fowl, and Somali ostrich. You will not encounter these species in other parks on typical photographic itineraries.

With daily critical editing you will know whether or not you have created satisfactory images of these specialty species. If not, you will be able to talk to your driver and to the other photographers in your vehicle. Show them your "shopping list" and see if you can all improve your images before it is time to move on to another game park.

After doing your edit, there will still be plenty of time for a nap, a swim, or a walk around the grounds to do some extra photography. A light lunch and some reading or a second nap will keep you refreshed for the afternoon game drive.

While it would seem to be desirable to be out in the game park as long as possible, you may find that this often results in a lot of hard work in harsh conditions with very little return if you choose the wrong times. If it is a cloudy afternoon, you can easily get out into the park around 3:00 pm. On an overcast day, the animals will be more active and the light will be less harsh than on a sunny day.

If it is a hot, blue-sky day, consider going out at 4:00 or even 4:30 pm when the animals will just be waking up from their afternoon siestas. Finding great subjects in the afternoon is typically a bit more difficult than it is in the morning. Most of the best action will be close to sundown.

As the sun nears the western horizon and the light is gorgeous, it can be very frustrating for photographers. As the light is just getting golden, your driver may tell you that it is time to go. Many of the parks have strict rules governing the times that the vans need to be off of the tracks and back at the lodges and camps; most game parks require that drivers return to the lodge no later than 6:30 pm or face the consequences. Over the years, I have learned to trust my drivers on this. They know exactly where they are in relation to the lodge and they know how long it will take to complete the return trip. This does not mean that you are finished; you never know what you might see on the way back. It is best to have your equipment ready so if you do make a stop for something great, it is likely to be a short one.

After getting back to my room or tent, I duplicate my routine of charging batteries and downloading cards. If I have time, I will edit the afternoon's images and then go to supper. Then it is time for relaxation and a sharing of the day's events.

Running wildebeest at dawn, Maasai Mara, Kenya

Running zebras, Maasai Mara, Kenya

Safari Tale #14

One evening we were far from the lodge photographing a nice group of zebras. The light was just OK and the photo opportunities limited. The driver said that it was time to go but some photographers wanted to stay. It was a classic case of "We are here photographing, so it must be good." I told them to trust the driver's decision. We were rewarded on the way home with a pair of lions right next to the road. There were lots of chances to make some wonderful close-up portraits. We did not have long, but in three minutes we all wound up with more keepers than we did after spending more than 45 minutes with the zebra herd.

Lesson:

Trust your driver.

Food and Lodging

When traveling to an exotic destination, it is only natural to have questions about what you will be photographing and what equipment you should bring. In addition, you may have questions about food and lodging. "What do I eat and where do I sleep?" are both valid concerns that will be addressed in this section.

While on safari, you are likely to stay in a variety of accommodations. There are safari lodges, bush lodges, safari camps, camp sites, and wilderness camping. Here I will deal with the first three possibilities. Staying at either a camp site or a wilderness camping area is not conducive to big lens digital safari photography.

Camping

Camping can make for a great East African experience, but in almost all cases the lack of a reliable supply of electricity is a major issue. You are not as likely to be comfortable or to get as much rest in a camp as you are at a safari lodge. Being tired and uncomfortable can get in the way of creating great photo images.

Different lodges and camps offer features that cater to different budgets. The quality of accommodations, amenities, service, and location of each facility affects the price of your safari.

Lodges

Whether old or new, expensive or budget priced, the majority of lodges in East Africa will be suitable for a photographer's needs. They will all have power in the rooms for charging your electronic equipment. They will all be within the boundaries, or on land adjoining a national park or reserve. Lodges will typically have a fence or wall that separates the compound from the surrounding countryside.

Most offer a swimming pool and a list of amenities similar to what you would expect to find in a major hotel, and there will always be a large staff eager to meet your needs. Rooms will have either 2 twin beds or a queen-sized bed. There may be a few larger rooms or suites that can accommodate a family.

If you have a problem walking long distances or if you can't carry your equipment very far, check with your tour operator before the safari. They can sometimes arrange for you to get a room that is close to the reception area. This will give you a shorter distance to walk from the room to the vehicle. If you do not have a room up front and need help with your equipment, contact the front desk and ask for a porter to assist you. Give the staff enough notice so that you and your gear can get to the vehicles in plenty of time for the game drive. Remember to tip the porter.

Camp sites

Camp sites offer the opportunity to be in prime locations at all times of the day or night. While these locations can put you in close proximity with beautiful scenery and wildlife, the inherent limitation of amenities (such as access to electrical power and a clean environment for equipment) are a terminal detriment to long lens digital safari photography.

Wilderness camps, northern Tanzania Photo © Brian Gustafson

At peak times of the safari season, lodges can become bustling beehives of activity. With lots of tourist groups and vans arriving and departing every day, there are a few tips to keep in mind. With all of the people (yourself included), there will be times when lots of suitcases and equipment are piled in the lobby. Make sure that you know where your cases and equipment are at all times. It is easy to come in from a long hot game drive and head straight for the bar and a cold drink, forgetting that you have set down your equipment in the lobby.

The drivers usually have separate parking areas and separate lodging facilities, usually but not always adjacent to the lodges. If you have a few items that you would like to leave in your vehicle overnight, ask the driver if it is safe to do so. If you forget something in a vehicle after a game drive, it can be difficult to track down the driver until the next game drive. It is a good idea to make sure that you take everything that you will need as you exit the vehicle after each game drive.

When you check out of a lodge, be sure to leave your room key. This tip alone can save your safari group hours; in the middle of the African wilderness; a key is not easily replaceable. The lodges are very serious about getting their missing keys back. If your room key is in your pocket while you are driving to the next lodge or to the airfield or airport, the lodge will radio your driver. The driver will have to make his way back to the lodge and begin the journey again. If this happens, it can be very upsetting to folks in the group, so do your best to remember to return your room key before leaving the lodge.

View of the Mara from Serena Lodge, Kenya

251

Bush Lodges

Bush lodges are almost always located right in the game parks and reserves. They are typically smaller than the safari lodges and have a more intimate feel to them. There are no fences; wildlife is often seen wandering on and through the grounds. There is also more of a family feel to the staff at a bush lodge. Staff members are usually local people who often work at the lodge for years.

A bush lodge campfire can be a magical experience. There are far fewer building lights at these smaller facilities and the stars are so thick that it sometimes feels as if there is a blanket across the sky. Take time away from your computer to sit with fellow travelers at the fire. The people you meet and the stories you hear can be life-changing.

Electricity at the bush lodges can be unreliable at times. Often, there are no outlets in the rooms and electricity is supplied by a generator. Ask the front desk when the generator is scheduled to be on. Sometimes the hours of operation do not coincide with the times when you are back at the lodge. Ask at the desk if there is a safe place to plug in a battery charger or a laptop while you are out on a game drive. Usually there is area near the front desk or by the bar where there will always be someone around to keep an eye on your equipment. For large safari groups, the management may even leave the generator on for a longer period of time as a courtesy, but you will never know unless you ask. (Hint: ask for their help, be polite, look needy).

The road to Ndudtu Bush Lodge, Ndutu, Tanzania

Ndutu Safari Lodge, Ndutu, Tanzania, Photo © Brian Gustafson

Permanent Tented Camps

Tented camping can have the romantic connotations of "being one with nature" or with "roughing it." The former may be true, but the latter is usually not the case. When staying at a permanent tented camp, you are definitely not "roughing it." The tents are built on poured cement floors or on raised wood platforms and are equipped with bathrooms that have a shower, a sink, and flush toilets. Other amenities include lights, a small desk, and often adequate storage space.

What is often missing from these tents are electrical outlets for powering or recharging your electronic gear. Desk lamps and overhead lights are usually hard wired to the tent's power box leaving photographers without a place to plug in. The solution to this is the same as at the bush lodge. Check at the front desk or the bar for a power outlet.

With groups of safari photographers needing power, and outlets in short supply, the best piece of equipment to bring with you is a Todd-Plug which allows you to power and/or charge multiple items at the same time while working from only a single outlet. Better yet, Todd-Plugs can be "daisy chained." With two of them you could power up as many as 14 chargers. Tented camps and bush lodges have similar generator issues. Find out from the front desk what the hours of operation are.

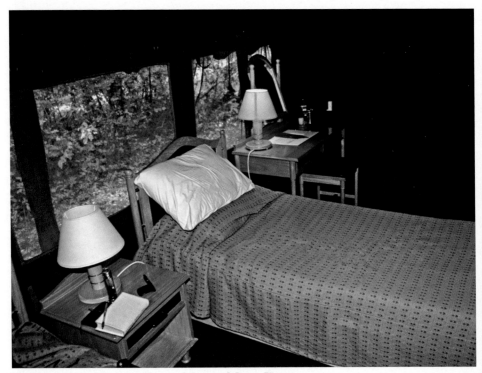

Tented camp bed, Sarova Camp, Maasai Mara, Kenya

Security is an important issue at tented camps. It is of vital importance that your tent flap is zipped all the way up whenever you leave, not to keep people from stealing your valuables but to prevent the local wildlife from stealing them. Vervet monkeys and troops of baboons are common around camps. They are smart, curious, and are not above raiding your tent to look for a free meal! They can do a lot of damage once they get inside of your tent. Any food that you leave in your tent such as bags of nuts, protein bars, or other snacks will be ruined and they may destroy or consume your irreplaceable medicines or supplements.

Camp fire at Ndutu Bush Lodge, Ndutu , Tanzania

Here is a courtesy tip:

If you bring a laptop computer out to the camp fire to do some editing, it may be practical for you, but the electric glow from the screen and tapping keys can ruin the ambience for the rest of those travelers around the fire. Likewise, a computer screen at the dinner table can be a distraction to both your table and those tables around you. It is difficult for other tables of travelers not to be curious about the images on the laptop screens. The ripple effect can disrupt the entire dining room. There is no escape for people trying to have a quiet dinner.

Leave the computer in your room.

Larson's Tented Camp, Samburu, Kenya

Tented camps

Tented camps are usually located in prime wildlife areas but are not always within national park or reserve borders. Some camps are situated outside of these borders by design and are not therefore subject to park rules and regulations. There are, for example, many permanent tented camps outside the borders of the Maasai Mara National Reserve. These camps are often located relatively near the great migration routes but are situated so as not to impact the movements of the wildebeest, zebras, and other herd animals. The animals do not recognize park boundaries.

A popular activity at some of these camps are night game drives that are prohibited inside of the parks. These game drives can enhance your safari experience. You will have a chance to view nocturnal animals that you might not normally see. Safari vehicles (outfitted with large floodlights), leave camp around 10:00 pm and wind through the bush searching for game, predators, and birds. Sometimes the animals freeze for several moments before they bolt into the darkness.

My view is that night game drives are not particularly interesting from a photographic point unless you are a specialist in infrared photography. I feel that the animals are disturbed by the harsh lights. I do not like intruding on their lives when they are at their most vulnerable.

Tarangire river valley, Tarangire, Tanzania

Elephants in Tarangire river valley, Tarangire, Tanzania

The view from a lodge or camp can be a huge factor in the selection of accommodations. For example, I do not like the lodges on the south end of Tarangire National Park in Tanzania. The Sopa Lodge is located in a valley, so it has no view. Tarangire Tented Camp (photo on right) is located on a bluff overlooking the river. This view of the drinking elephant herd was taken from the path to the tent area.

Right: Elephants in Tarangire river, Tarangire, Tanzania

Food

"What am I going to eat?" is an often-asked question before most safaris even begin. My answer is "Lots of good food!" The lodges and camps all have trained chefs and kitchen staffs eager to provide you with good meals. Most of the lodges and camps have their own gardens so the vegetables are fresh. Chicken, beef, and fish are usually on the dinner menu.

Fresh fruit is also abundant, and the breads and rolls are always freshly baked. Sodas, local beers, and mixed drinks are always available as are coffee and tea. The east African coffee and tea are fantastic and make great gifts for folks back home. You can purchase them at a variety of locations while on safari.

Lodges and camps serve meals in a wide variety of styles. Meals chosen from a menu may be alternated with buffet-style dinners. At Lake Nakuru Lodge an outdoor barbecue can usually be arranged. There is usually a cheese tray and a desert selection after the main meal. Some lodges offer a pasta bar at most dinners.

Now a word about boxed meals. Boxed breakfasts usually contain some fruit, a hard boiled egg, a juice box and several variations of breakfast pastries. They will also have either sausages or bacon. In my view, they are not the greatest meal in the history of the world, but they will get you through the morning.

I love having a full breakfast at the lodge but if the primary goal is to make great pictures, eating a full breakfast will take time away from game drives. Realize that while you are eating your boxed breakfast you are in the middle of one of the most exciting photographic destinations on the planet! Make full use of this precious time. There will be travel days where you will be able partake of a sumptuous lodge breakfast.

If you are a salad lover, I have bad news for you. Eat the fresh vegetables and the salad greens at your own risk. The ground that they grow in has microorganisms that our systems are not adapted to cope with; the lettuce and tomatoes are washed with water that may influence your stomach in a manner that will not likely be pleasing. All freshly picked local produce may be a potential health hazard. I recommend that only cooked vegetables or fruit that can be peeled be eaten. There have been people on my safaris that have eaten salads and fresh vegetables with no reported bad side effects, but they are few and far between. Others have suffered for a day or two or even more. I do not eat the salads and I tend not to get sick. I leave the choice up to you.

Right: Lunch buffet, Sarova Camp, Maasai Mara, Kenya

Safari Tale #15

In 2006 I entered the BBC Wildlife Photographer of the Year and won a prize for Runner Up in the Bird Behavior category. This was very exciting, even more so when I learned that there had been more than 18,000 entries in the competition. I include this information here because the creation of the honored image incorporated many of the concepts covered in this book. When people see a stunning nature photograph, many of them think "Boy, you sure were lucky to get that picture."

Here are the conscious choices that I made that led to my getting the "lucky shot."

Professional quality camera equipment the Canon EOS-1D Mark II camera body and the Canon EF 600mm f/4L I lens.

Adequate camera support: The Todd-Pod and Wimberley head enabled me to make a sharp image with my chosen equipment.

Perspective and position: I laid flat on the ground fairly close to the birds. This provided a lovely background of uncluttered grays and soft pinks.

Photographic technique: I chose a wide aperture, had a steadying hand resting on the lens barrel, and squeezed the release button slowly.

Quality data storage: I used a 4 gig SanDisc Ultra lll compact flash card; I have found them fast and reliable.

Dependable safari company: I chose a company that had reliable, high quality vehicles and experienced, knowledgeable drivers.

Location: I included Lake Nakuru on our itinerary primarily because flamingos tend to abound there in summer. I had noted previously that the small peninsula where I chose to set up afforded a great light-angle in early morning with the light coming directly over my head and illuminating the Lesser Flamingoes perfectly.

Subject and behavior: Stands of flamingoes will typically feature birds exhibiting courtship behavior such as the mating dance seen here.

Time of day: On clear mornings at Nauru I almost always head down to the lake before dawn to be in position when the sun first comes over the distant hills providing soft, warmly colored light. .

Lesson: *The harder I work, the luckier I get.*

"Flamingo Dance"
Lake Nakuru, Kenya August 2005
2006 BBC Wildlife Photographer of the Year Runner up, Bird Behavior

Conclusion

As you have discovered by reading this far, there are many factors to consider when planning a photographic safari to East Africa. My hope is that what you have read will help you to formulate a photographic strategy that will prepare you for your safari to the wilds of East Africa.

By getting the right equipment and taking care of it, by applying what you have learned here, and by developing new photographic skills, you will be able to create many pleasing, memorable, and dramatic images on your safari. By making decisions based on the information contained in the various sections of this book, you will likely be well prepared to fulfill your photographic visions and dreams.

I love East Africa and it is my hope that this book will help you have an enjoyable and productive photo safari. If you have any questions, if there are any subjects that you feel were not covered here, or if you would like additional information on a topic, please feel free to e-mail me at:

gustaphoto@aol.com

The End

Common Zebra, Maasai Mara, Kenya

Resources

Photographic Equipment

Arthur Morris/BIRDS AS ART www.birdsasart.com
Instructional photo tours Specialty nature photography equipment
Inspirational/Educational; honest critiques done gently:
www.BirdPhotographers.Net

Calumet Photographic www.calumetphoto.com
Full line pro photography equipment sales
Instructional seminars
Studio lighting
(800)CALUMET (225-8638)

Micronet Computers
Custom built PC equipment
(847)470-0890

United Camera Repair
Authorised Nikon and Canon repair service
(630)595-2525

Wimberly Products
www.tripodhead.com
(888)665-2746

Appendix

Upcoming projects from Gustafson Photo Safari

Companion books on CD

Sight Guide to East African Game Parks is a park-by-park guide to many of the best safari photo destinations in Kenya, Tanzania, Zanzibar and Madagascar. Included are shooting strategies for different locations in the parks specific to time of day, direction of light, etc. Specialty species for each park are discussed in detail.

Areas included:

Tanzania-Country Review
•Arusha National Park
•Tarangire
•Lake Manyara
•Serengeti
•Ngorongoro Crater
•Ngorongoro Conservation Area (NCA)

Kenya-Country Review
•Amboseli
•Tsavo
•Lake Nakuru
•Maasai Mara National Reserve
•Samburu/Buffalo Springs National Reserve
•Rift Valley Lakes
     •Lake Naivasha
     •Lake Baringo
     •Lake Bogoria

Indian Ocean Coast and under water Indian Ocean
•Mombasa
•South Coast
•North Coast
•Malindi
•Gedi Ruins

Madagascar

Bamburi Nature Trail

Bamburi is a miracle of regenerative conservation. The culmination of a Swiss conservationist's work, Bamburi has been transformed from a desolate cement mining operation into a lush, tropical nature reserve. From 1970s to the present the goal of the Bamburi Conservation program has been to use nature's own power to convert and sustain this coastal oasis. Australian pine saplings were planted and thousands of millipedes were brought to the area to eat and recycle the fallen pine leaves. Fertile soil covers the area as a result and supports a thriving tropical ecosystem.

Walking along the light dappled paths you can easily find millipedes in all sizes. Locals call them "Mombasa Trains" because the ground speed of this millipede is about the same speed as an East African locomotive (very often slower than a crawl). The speed can be deceptively fast when you try to photograph them. To get an interesting curve you will need a high f stop for the necessary. A high ISO will help as will the use of an off camera flash.

As you enter the grounds, look for some of the resident giant Aldabra tortoise. Several of these huge reptiles have been imported from Aldabra Atoll in the Seychelles Islands. The grounds are kept trimmed by these approachable giants. Ground level shots are a good approach, since they feed low to the ground on their flat undershells. Try using fill flash to throw some light under the chin and the underside of the animal.

On the way up the path walking toward the beautifully thatched visitor's center look to the right. There is a series of pools and marshes where you can easily photograph the pied kingfishers, who nest in the banks as they fly, dive, hover and perch on the papyrus that line the banks.

The nature trail has plenty of photogenic subjects, some captive, some free and wild. In the main compound there is a lily-covered pond where you can photograph hippos yawning and fighting at eye level. The angle of view is dramatic and the green of the lily pads adds a rich, appealing flavor. Other animals in this area are water buck and a nice herd of eland. Crowned cranes, white egret, grey heron and Goliath heron also frequent the pond.

Along the shaded paths you can photograph crocodile filled pools, giraffe and oryx in clearings and vervet monkeys everywhere. Keep your eyes open around the main crocodile pools for golden palm-weavers. They build their nests in this area because the crocs keep it relatively predator free.

There is a reptile house where you can view snakes that are usually difficult to see in the wild. It's pretty dark in there and the habitats are not very photogenic. However, you can talk to your guide about having a handler remove some of the non-venomous species for photography. I have even had a guide drain a tilapia pool so that I could photograph the fish for the Lincoln Park Zoo Africa Exhibit in Chicago. The guide chose a fish for me to photograph and held it up in beautiful light. After the photograph he refilled the pool, slipped the chosen fish into a bucket and took it home for dinner.

East African Animal and Bird Behavior is a Book on CD guide to animal behavior written specifically with the photographer in mind. It will discuss behaviors that you would likely see and want to photograph as well as specific locations where they are most common and, more importantly, best for photography. There are techniques and strategies discussed that will allow you to better anticipate the peak moment of action.

Some of the species covered include:

Animals
Giraffe
Zebra
Elephant
Black Rhino
White Rhino
Hippo
Oryx
Water buck
Eland
Sable
Gazelles
Gerenuk
Dik-dik
Lion
Leopard
Cheetah
Genet
Serval Cat

Birds

There are just under 1,300 bird species in Kenya and Tanzania. I am in no way a "Birder." I have, however, spent countless hours photographing birds in East Africa. My brother Brian and I long ago developed the philosophy that on safari you WILL see elephants, lions and giraffes. If that is all you are interested in you will have a shallower and less rewarding safari. If you can appreciate the number and variety of bird species to see and photograph you will enhance the safari experience In this chapter I obviously can't discuss them all so I have chosen the ones that a photographer would be likely to encounter or those that especially interest me photographically, behaviorally and visually. If you have species that you would like to know about that I have not covered here please contact me at gustaphoto@aol.com and I will do my best to help you.

Flight
Perched
Wading
Flamingos
Raptors
Sun birds
Bush birds
Bee-eaters
Barbets
Weaver birds
Pelicans
Kingfishers
Avocets
Stilts
Jacanas
Plovers
Cranes
Storks
Rollers

Reptiles

Though there are many classes of reptiles in East Africa, many are nocturnal or shy. This section will provide information about species that are likely to be seen during daylight hours. They include:

Crocodile
Nile monitor lizards
Red agama lizards
Green agama lizards
Skinks
Chameleons
Snakes

Safari Tale

When I was in Bamburi with Arthur Morris, the discussion of "pinioning" (clipping the flight feathers of birds to keep the in the compound) arose. Art asked our local guide if the birds pinioned.

The guide answered "Yes, they are pinioned."

Art then asked "So, the birds can't fly away?"

The guide answered "Yes, they can fly away. They are free to come and go."

The conversation deteriorated from there...

"Are they pinioned?"

The guide said "No."

Can they come and go?"

The guide said "No."

There was obviously some sort of communication problem. It got so bad that Art ended up asking the guide if the Mosquitoes were pinioned!!!

Lesson: *Know when cultural differences make it wise to give up on a situation and move on.*

Notes

Notes

Notes

Notes

Notes

Notes

Notes